BIBLE
SERMON
OUTLINES

BIBLE SERMON OUTLINES

Ian Macpherson

ABINGDON PRESS
Nashville   New York

BIBLE SERMON OUTLINES

Copyright © 1966 by Abingdon Press

Library of Congress Catalog Card Number: 66-12926

"For the Fallen" by Laurence Binyon (quoted
No. 62) used by permission of the Society of
Authors.
Lines from "The Divine Tragedy" by Arthur St.
John Adcock (quoted No. 229) used by permission
of Hodder and Stoughton.
Lines from "Indifference," from Sorrows of God
by Geoffrey A. Studdert-Kennedy (quoted No. 229)
used by permission of Harper & Row, Publishers,
Inc.
Lines from "Easter Night" by Alice Meynell
(quoted No. 300) used by permission of Charles
Scribner's Sons.
"Tetelestai" (No. 305) from Teaching and
Preaching the New Testament by Archibald M.
Hunter. © SMC Press Ltd., 1963. Published
U. S. A. 1963, The Westminster Press. Used by
permission.
"I Keep Six Honest Serving Men" (quoted No.
390) from The Elephant's Child by Rudyard Kip-
ling. Reprinted by permission of Mrs. George
Bambridge and Doubleday & Company, Inc., and
Macmillan Company of Canada, Ltd.
"In Trouble and Shame" (quoted No. 422) from
The Complete Poems of D. H. Lawrence; copy-
right 1920 by B. W. Heubsch, Inc., 1947 by Frieda
Lawrence; reprinted by permission of The Viking
Press, Inc.
"Orthodox" by Mark Guy Pearse (quoted No.
488) from Masterpieces of Religious Verse; re-
printed by permission of Harper & Row, Publishers,
Inc.

SET UP, PRINTED, AND BOUND BY THE
PARTHENON PRESS, AT NASHVILLE,
TENNESSEE, UNITED STATES OF AMERICA

PREFACE

Years ago in Scotland I used to know an old man who, with a mischievous twinkle in his eye, would sometimes deliberately misquote a text of Scripture. "Now the works of the flesh are manifest," he would say, "which are these—preaching!"

He felt, presumably, that there were preachers who made a god of their own words instead of humbly communicating the Word of God. When that happens, preaching does indeed become a work of the flesh.

Such a collection of sermon outlines as this might perhaps convey the impression that preaching is very largely a work of bones! And Clovis G. Chappell has told us that "a book of 'skeletons' is about the most useless of all boneyards."

Nevertheless, high moments come in the ministry of every preacher when the miracle recorded in II Kings 13:21 is repeated: "It came to pass, as they were burying a man, that, behold, they spied a band of men; and they cast the man into the sepulchre of Elisha: and when the man was let down, and the man touched the bones of Elisha, he revived, and stood up on his feet." Prophetic "bones" possess vitalizing potency, and homiletic stimulus may be derived from the "skeletons" of buried sermons.

Only, of course, they have to be the "bones" of true prophets! All other "bones" are best left interred. There is nothing particularly animating in some forms of ossified sermonizing! Every genuine Elisha, however, is electrifying. Even his "bones" impart a vital spark.

Consider these instances.

Here, to begin with, is the "skeleton" of a discourse by an old prophet on Gen. 28:12: "And he [Jacob] dreamed, and behold a ladder set up on the earth, and the top of it reached to heaven: and behold the angels of God ascending and descending on it." With his vivid pictorial imagination, the preacher watched those shining beings moving up and down the mystic ladder, and, with a touch of genius, he named them thus:

1. *Aspiration and Inspiration.*
2. *Inquiry and Revelation.*
3. *Effort and Enablement.*

What preacher worth his salt does not leap to sudden sermonic life upon touching "bones" like these?

Or take the "bones" of an address by another prophet. Basing his discourse on John 3:16, "For God so loved the world, that he gave his only begotten Son, that whosoever believeth in him should not perish, but have everlasting life," he skillfully articulated the following marrowy "skeleton":

1. The fact.
   "For God so loved the world."

5

2. The act.
   "That he gave his only begotten Son."
3. The pact.
   "That whosoever believeth in him should not perish, but have everlasting life."

Is there a Christian minister with the least trace of homiletic sensibility who does not experience a mental quickening as he reads that?

The point to notice in the miracle, however, is that it was not Elisha who came to life again, but the dead man who touched Elisha's bones. The prophet was not himself resuscitated. Nor are the sermon plans in this compilation meant to be lifted bodily out of the book and used as the bases of new sermons. They are intended to be taken as models by masters of the craft. They are designed not to *spare* the preacher but to *spur* him.

Joseph Parker, a famous London preacher of a former day, once said: "Give me Delitzsch, and I will Matthew Henry-ize for myself"—which, being interpreted, is: "Give me the findings of biblical scholarship, and I will draw up my own diagrams of discourse." Well, we are profoundly grateful for any fresh light that scholarship can cast on the sacred page: but surely if the scholars can help us to understand the Scriptures the preachers can help us to expound them! The student of preaching can no more afford to ignore the study of the sermon outlines of sermon masters than the student of medicine or of art can afford to ignore the study of the structure of the human body. This collection of plans is offered as a modest manual of homiletic anatomy.

To get the best out of the book the reader would be well advised to adopt the following procedure. First, let him turn to the textual index and choose from it some suitable passage of Scripture. Next let him examine the text closely, using such literary aids as lie at hand in the form of lexicons, commentaries, etc.; and looking up the exact meaning in the original Scripture, relate it livingly to its biblical background.

Then let him ask himself to what type of treatment the text is likely to be most amenable—the synthetic or the analytic, the topical or the expository. (Incidentally, the synthetic may be said to resemble the growth of a baby in the womb; the analytic, the dissection of a corpse on an autopsy table.)

Having made up his mind on that issue, let him block out the plan, wording the points as tersely and as tellingly as he can, placing them in proper logical order and climactic sequence, and working on them until he feels about them as a poet does about the finished verse which he gives to the world.

After that, let him pick up this volume once more, refer to the relevant page and note how the text is handled there. And finally, let him compare his own plan with that in the compilation, observing correspondences and contrasts between them, and trying thereby to improve his craftsmanship.

6

CONTENTS
Old Testament

New Testament

Old
Testament

GENESIS

1. SERPENTS

"Now the serpent was more subtile than any beast of the field which the Lord God had made."
Gen. 3:1

"And as Moses lifted up the serpent in the wilderness, even so must the Son of man be lifted up."
John 3:14

"And I saw an angel coming down from heaven, having the key of the bottomless pit and a great chain in his hand. And he laid hold on the dragon, that old serpent, which is the Devil, and Satan, and bound him a thousand years, and cast him into the bottomless pit." Rev. 20:1-3a

The Bible has a good deal to say about serpents. There is a reference to a serpent at its beginning; there is a reference to a serpent in its middle; and there is a reference to a serpent at its close. And all the way through, from Genesis to Revelation, the Scriptures make us conscious that there is a snake in the grass of human history and of the human heart!

It is about three of these biblical allusions to serpents that I want to speak now.

The serpent! Is there an uglier, more hideous, sinister, repulsive creature on earth than a serpent? Its cold, coiled sliminess; its beady, mesmeric, unlidded eye; its blood-curdling hiss; its stealthy, surreptitious movements; its swiftness in attack; its poisoned fang—all conspire to make it the most loathsome and detestable of living things!

Herpetologists—that is, those who make a special study of reptiles—have estimated that before the comparatively modern discovery of a cure for snake-poisoning, some 20,000 people died of it every year in India alone! And as there are between 1,500 and

11

1,800 species of serpents infesting the hot belt of the world—Africa, India, Australia, South America—they must be responsible for the death annually of thousands.

Not as the cause of natural death, however, but as that of spiritual death is the serpent mainly spoken of in Scripture. Consider:

1. The serpent allowed in.

It is highly significant that, according to the Bible, sin began not among the animals—where one might have expected it to begin—but among the angels; not in the depths of existence, but in its heights; not among the lower orders of creation, but among the highest order of created beings.

Sin made its nest among the stars.

"I beheld Satan as lightning fall from heaven."
Luke 10:18

2. The "serpent" lifted up.

Here we must enclose the word "serpent" in quotation marks. A brass serpent cannot bite you. As Matthew Henry's commentary puts it:

It [the brazen serpent] was made in the shape of a fiery serpent, and yet had no poison, no sting, fitly representing Christ, who was made sin for us, and yet knew no sin; was made in the likeness of sinful flesh, and yet not sinful. The serpent is a cursed creature: Christ was made a curse for us.

3. The serpent cast down.

The snake, one instinctively feels, is a creature that ought not to exist. George Bernard Shaw said that. He declared that whenever he saw a snake he had an immediate impulse to scotch it.

I wonder who invented the game of snakes and ladders. Whoever he may have been, he certainly displayed discernment and insight in his choice of symbols. Always the way up to heaven is like a ladder; always the way down to hell is by a snake!

Because Christ, as the "serpent," was lifted up, that old serpent, the Devil, will at last be cast down.

2. THORNS

1. Thorns of ruin.
"Thorns also and thistles shall it bring forth to thee."
Gen. 3:18

2. Thorns of redemption.
"Then came Jesus forth, wearing the crown of thorns, and the purple robe."
John 19:5

3. Thorns of regeneration.
"Instead of the thorn shall come up the fir tree, and instead of the brier shall come up the myrtle tree: and it shall be to the Lord for a name, for an everlasting sign that shall not be cut off."
Isa. 55:13

—George Henderson,
Lectures to Young Preachers

3. MY BROTHER'S KEEPER

"And the Lord said unto Cain, Where is Abel thy brother? And he said, I know not: Am I my brother's keeper?" Gen. 4:9

Here, right at the beginning, the Bible insists upon our social responsibilities.

Note that:

1. We are responsible for every member of our family.
2. We are responsible for every member of Christ's church.
3. We are responsible for every member of the human race.

—Gerald B. Griffiths,
My Brother's Keeper

4. A BRIEF BIOGRAPHY

"All the days of Enoch were three hundred sixty and five years: and Enoch walked with God: and he was not; for God took him."
Gen. 5:23, 24

It is really a matter of fact that the good do not always die young, as some sentimental people would have us believe.

Enoch is a standing proof of that.

Look at:

1. His companionship.
   He felt lonely and wanted a friend who could enter into his heart and life as only God could.
2. His surroundings.
   He lived at a very bad time in the history of the world.
3. His activity.
   His life was a busy one, and he had all the cares of a large family.

4. His progress.
   He walked with God. And one day he took a longer walk than usual and never returned.

—John Mitchell, *Stones for Sermon Builders*

5. WHY GOD'S SPIRIT CEASES TO STRIVE

"My Spirit shall not always strive with man." Gen. 6:3

Life provides us with many examples of the strong striving with the weak that the weak may become strong. From the lioness struggling with her cubs in the jungle to the schoolmaster wrestling with the minds of his pupils in the classroom, there are many illustrations of this.

So the Spirit of God strives with the souls of men. He struggles with us, as the angel wrestled with Jacob, in order that we may grow strong. Our text warns us, however, that a point may be reached in the relations of the divine with the human at which the Holy Spirit ceases thus to strive.

Consider four instances of this, as exemplified in the biographies of the Bible, and note in each case why it came about.

1. Take Samson.
   Why did the Spirit of God cease to strive with him? Because of *sensuality.* "God . . . gave them up." Rom. 1:24
2. Take Saul.
   Why did the Spirit of God cease to strive with him? Because of *disobedience.* "Rebel-

13

lion is as the sin of witchcraft, and stubbornness is as iniquity and idolatry. Because thou hast rejected the word of the Lord, he hath also rejected thee from being king."

I Sam. 15:23

3. Take Solomon.
Why did the Spirit of God cease to strive with him? Because of *idolatry*. "It came to pass, when Solomon was old, that his wives turned away his heart after other gods: and his heart was not perfect with the Lord his God, as was the heart of David his father." I Kings 11:4

4. Take Judas.
Why did the Spirit of God cease to strive with him? Because of *avarice* and *dishonesty*. "He was a thief, and had the bag, and bare what was put therein." John 12:6 "He went his way, and communed with the chief priests and captains, how he might betray him unto them. And they were glad, and covenanted to give him money."

Luke 22:4, 5

Still as of old
Men by themselves are priced—
For thirty pieces Judas sold
Himself, not Christ.
—Hester H. Cholmondeley

A young man went once to a minister of Christ in great distress of mind. "The Holy Spirit has left me," he said. The minister sought to persuade him otherwise, reminding him of the long-suffering of the Spirit of God. But the young man was not to be convinced. "Isn't there a text somewhere," he asked, "to the effect that 'God's Spirit will not always strive with man'?" "There is," admitted the minister. "It is Genesis 6:3." "Well," went on the youth, "he has ceased to strive with me." "However did that happen?" inquired the minister solicitously. "It was like this," the young man explained. "For months the Spirit of God had been striving with me, urging me—almost pestering me, you might say—to surrender to Christ. At last my patience was exhausted, and I exclaimed: "O Holy Spirit, go away. I do not want to be bothered with you any longer." "And," said the young man, "He did! He did! I haven't once been conscious of his striving since that day."

Stay, Thou insulted Spirit, stay!
Though I have done Thee such
despite,
Nor cast the sinner quite away,
Nor take Thine everlasting flight.
—Charles Wesley

6. THE BOW IN THE CLOUD

"I do set my bow in the cloud, and it shall be for a token of a covenant between me and the earth."

Gen. 9:13

Note:

1. It is a bow without an arrow.
2. It is a bow turned away from the earth.
3. It is a bow bright with beauty against a background of black clouds.

7. THE TWO RAINBOWS

"Behold, I do set my bow in the cloud." Gen. 9:13
"There was a rainbow round about the throne." Rev. 4:3

There is something strikingly suggestive in the fact that at the beginning and at the end of the Bible mention is made of a rainbow.
Think of one or two facts about a rainbow.

1. A rainbow is woven of storm and sunshine.
   It is threaded by the bright fingers of the sunshine on the loom of the rain.
2. A rainbow is always turned away from the earth.
   A friend of mine, a Swiss nurse, told me of one of the most moving and memorable moments in her professional career. It was in Switzerland. She was at the time attending a fine old Christian man in his last illness. For him, death was not so much a physical ordeal as a spiritual experience. As the end drew near, his face became absolutely radiant. She watched him closely, alone with him in the little private cubicle. Suddenly, she saw life fade from his face. Behind him was a window. Through it she could see the sunny sky laced by a shower. Like a halo framing the head of the dead saint was a beautiful rainbow.
   She felt it was symbolic.
3. Earth's rainbow is always a broken arc: heaven's is a perfect round.

The pilot of an airplane once surprised a minister by asking: "Have you ever seen the rainbow as a full circle?" "No," replied the minister, "there is no such thing. A rainbow is always an arc." "On the contrary," went on the pilot, "when riding high in the heavens in my aircraft I have often seen the rainbow as a perfect circle." Then the minister remembered Rev. 4:3.

8. GOD'S ESPERANTO

"The whole earth was . . . of one speech." Gen. 11:1

The most important of the many attempts to invent an artificial language, Esperanto, was devised by L. L. Zamenhof (1859-1917), a Jewish oculist living in Poland, who gave it to the world in 1887. The name Esperanto is adapted from the Spanish word for hope, *esperanza.* The new composite language is justifying its name. It is spreading rapidly throughout the nations. Nearly a hundred textbooks on it in different languages have been issued. Scores of magazines are printed in it and thousands of books published.

Now, God too has his Esperanto. Consider the following three relevant biblical references:

1. Confusion of tongues.
   "The Lord did there confound the language." Gen. 11:9
2. Effusion of tongues.
   "There appeared unto them cloven tongues like as of fire. . . . And they were all filled

15

with the Holy Ghost, and began to speak with other tongues." Acts 2:4
3. Fusion of tongues.
"They sung a new song, saying, Thou . . . hast redeemed us to God by thy blood out of every . . . tongue." Rev. 5:9

9. SYMBOLS OF THE HOLY SEED

"I will make thy seed as the dust of the earth." Gen. 13:16
"I will multiply thy seed as the stars of the heaven." Gen. 22:17
"I will . . . make thy seed as the sand of the sea." Gen. 32:12

Doubtless the primary purpose behind the employment of these figures of speech in the divine promise to Abraham was to impress upon the mind of the patriarch the number of those who were to form his progeny.

May we not, however, without being too fanciful, find other suggestions here?

Surely the Jews are:
1. Like the dust in their lowliness.

"Hath not a Jew eyes? hath not a Jew hands, organs, dimensions, senses, affections, passions? fed with the same food, hurt with the same weapons, subject to the same diseases, healed by the same means, warmed and cooled by the same winter and summer, as a Christian is?"

—Shakespeare,
The Merchant of Venice

2. Like the stars in their changelessness.

Someone has said that the Jews in history have been like Jonah in the whale—unassimilable!

3. Like the sand in their restlessness.
What nation on earth has been so tossed about as have the Jews on the tides of time?

10. NOTHING TOO HARD FOR THE LORD

"Is any thing too hard for the Lord?" Gen. 18:14

Observe that:
1. Things too hard for us are easy for other creatures.
   a) We can't fly; birds can.
   b) We can't carry our houses on our backs; snails can.

The little snail, so small and black,
Carries its house upon its back:
   But could Brezhnev do it?
   Could Johnson do it?
   Could Wilson do it?
   Why, no!

   c) We can't live for long under water; fishes can.
2. Things easy to us are too hard for other creatures.
   a) We can sing; cows can't.
   b) We can write; geese can't —though they do produce quills!
   c) We can walk; snakes can't.
3. Things too hard for us are easy to God.
   We must not ever measure his omnipotence by our impotence.
4. Things too hard for us are easy to us through God!

11. THE GREAT PROPOSAL

(A Wedding Sermon)
"Wilt thou go with this man?"
Gen. 24:58

It is always a wonderful moment in a woman's life when a man proposes marriage to her. Some beautiful young ladies, it is said, actually boast of the number of such proposals they have had, as the Indian warriors used to boast of the number of scalps they had collected! When one attractive spinster was asked how many suitors had sued for her hand, she is reported to have replied: "I have had ten *disposals*!"

In our text we have what must surely be the strangest proposal on record. Think of it. Rebekah was requested by a man she hardly knew to marry a man she had never met in a land she had never seen! That was, as we say, a tall order.

And there was so much to induce Rebekah to say "No." She was happy in Nahor. It was her ancestral home, and so forth.

Moreover, Rebekah was expected to move out on the mere word of Abraham's servant.

She did not hesitate. Believing the report, she made answer: "I will go." Gen. 24:58

I want you to notice six things about the proposal and reflect on how remarkably they correspond to the evangelical appeal.

1. It was voluntary, not compulsory.
   "Wilt thou?" not "Thou shalt!"
2. It was personal, not transferable.
   "Wilt *thou* go?"
3. It was active, not passive.
   "Wilt thou *go?*" not "Wilt thou *stay* with this man?"
4. It was specific, not indefinite.
   "Wilt thou go with *this* man?"—not somebody else!
5. It was companionable, not solitary.
   "Wilt thou go *with*—not after or before—this man?"
6. It was urgent, not deferrable.
   The question called for an immediate answer. She had no time to think it over. There and then she had to make up her mind. Was it to be "Yes" or "No"? The issue could not be postponed. The camels were loaded for the journey. The caravan was about to start. Her response was eagerly awaited. It soon came. "I will go."

So is it between your soul and Christ. What will your answer be? "Wilt thou go with this Man?"

12. THE ANGELS ON JACOB'S LADDER

"And he [Jacob] dreamed, and behold a ladder set up on the earth, and the top of it reached to heaven: and behold the angels of God ascending and descending on it."
Gen. 28:12

What were the names of those angels?

Here are some suggestions:

1. Aspiration and Inspiration.
2. Inquiry and Revelation.
3. Effort and Enablement.

—Unknown

17

13. BACK TO BETHEL

"I am the God of Bethel, where thou anointedst the pillar, and where thou vowedst a vow unto me: now arise, get thee out from this land, and return unto the land of thy kindred. Gen. 31:13

There are times when to go back is to go forward. Jacob had certainly gone forward in many ways since that now distant day when in his dreams he had seen the traffic of the shining ladder.

He had gone forward financially. Then he had been an impecunious vagabond. If there had been pennies and if he had had pockets, he would not have possessed one to put in the other. Now he was rich and prosperous, owner of flocks and herds, cattle being better currency than coin in the desert! Yes, he had gone forward financially.

He had gone forward socially too. Then he had been a solitary fugitive, a lone figure fleeing across the trackless hills. Now he was married and had a large family, as well as numerous servants. "Two bands" he calls his caravan. He had gone forward socially.

But had he gone forward in the most important sense—morally and spiritually? Was he a better man than he had been? Was his character keeping pace with his career? As a man of the world, he was getting on famously; but had he become a man of that other world which had blazed in on him that night in the long ago as he slept beneath the stars, with moss for a mattress and stone for a pillow?

No! It could not honestly be said that he had gone forward in that

18

way, and so he must go back—back to Bethel, back to the place of the anointed pillar and the solemn vow!

1. What a mercy we find Bethels on our pilgrimage!
2. What a pity we must leave our Bethels as we proceed on our pilgrimage!
3. What a blessing that, however far we may have wandered, there is always a way back to Bethel!

Sings Philip Doddridge:

O God of Bethel, by whose hand
Thy people still are fed;
Who through this weary pilgrimage
Hast all our fathers led:
Our vows, our prayers we now present
Before Thy throne of grace;
God of our fathers, be the God
Of their succeeding race.

14. AT THE CROSSING

(A New Year's Sermon)

"He [Jacob] . . . passed over the ford Jabbok." Gen. 32:22
"The children of Israel walked upon dry land in the midst of the sea." Exod. 14:29
"At the passages of Jordan." Judg. 12:6
"The Israelites passed over on dry ground." Josh. 3:17

It is always interesting, and sometimes exciting, to come to a great crossing. There are crossings a man may make which he will remember for a lifetime—the crossing of the Equator, the crossing of the Atlantic, the crossing of the Iron Curtain or the Berlin Wall.

All these are crossings in space. But there are crossings in time as well—the crossing of birth, the crossing of conversion, the crossing of marriage, the crossing of death.

Every New Year is such a crossing, and at this season we may profitably remind ourselves of four of the great crossings of the Bible.

Let us learn:

1. How fear found forgiveness at the crossing.
   Gen. 32:22-32
2. How faith found fulfillment at the crossing.
   Exod. 14:21-31
3. How fugitives were found false at the crossing.
   Judg. 12:4
4. How fortitude found firmness at the crossing.
   Josh. 3:10-17

15. WHEN VOWS ARE RENEWED

"And God said unto Jacob, Arise, go up to Bethel, and dwell there: and make there an altar unto God, that appeared unto thee when thou fleddest from the face of Esau thy brother." Gen. 35:1

Bethel! What happens there?

1. Guilt meets grace.
2. Loneliness meets love.
3. Dreams meet reality.

16. MISTAKEN ESTIMATE

"We are true men." Gen. 42:11

Were they? They spoke for themselves; they spoke for one another: but did they speak the truth? You know they did not—they were not true men; they were anything but true men.

Why do men now form similarly false estimates of themselves? Because:

1. They dwell on their superficial goodness and forget their deeper wickedness.
   That is what Joseph's brothers did. "We are not spies."
2. They dwell on their exceptional goodness and forget their prevailing wickedness.
   That, again, is what Joseph's brothers did.
3. They dwell on their present goodness and forget their past wickedness.
   That, once more, is what Joseph's brothers did.

But note the painful and shameful exposure. Every false self-estimate will be rectified at last by God's ruthless revelation of the facts!

—W. L. Watkinson,
The Bane and the Antidote

EXODUS

17. SHORTCUTS NOT GOD'S

"God led them not through the way of the land of the Philistines, although that was near."
Exod. 13:17

Here we have one feature of God's guidance. It shuns the near road and takes the roundabout.

1. Think of the discovery of nature's secrets—coal, iron, electricity.

A single whisper from God would have communicated everything and put mankind in possession of the secrets. But God never led us that way, though it was near.
2. Think of the coming of Jesus. Surely, in response to the world's need, he might have come a thousand years before! But God had no near way to Bethlehem.
3. Think of the evangelizing of the world.
By the slow method of individual conversion, one here and another there, the great work is going on.

—George H. Morrison,
Sunrise

18. THREE SORTS OF PEOPLE ON THE DESERT MARCH

"Speak unto the children of Israel, that they go forward."
Exod. 14:15
1. One group wanted to go back to Egypt.
They preferred slavery to the uncertainty of the wilderness.
2. The second group was satisfied wherever they might be at night.
They were content to gather the manna as it came.
3. The third group, the smallest, wanted to go forward.
Moses was among this number.

—John Haynes Holmes

19. A DAY'S PORTION

"A day's portion every day."
Exod. 16:4 RSV

1. Daily provision
"Give us this day our daily bread." Matt. 6:11
2. Daily care.
"Sufficient unto the day is the evil thereof." Matt. 6:34
3. Daily toil.
4. Daily grace.
—James Dinwoodie,
One Hundred Illustrated Outlines and Texts (adapted)

20. HEREDITY

"I the Lord thy God am a jealous God, visiting the iniquity of the fathers upon the children unto the third and upon the fourth generation of them that hate me; and showing mercy unto thousands of them that love me and keep my commandments." Exod. 20:5, 6
Consider:
1. The bane of heredity.
"Visiting the iniquity of the fathers upon the children."
2. The boon of heredity.
"Showing mercy unto thousands."
3. The break with heredity.
"Therefore if any man be in Christ, he is a new creature: old things are passed away; behold, all things are become new." II Cor. 5:17
—Unknown

21. THE LAW OF PROPERTY

"Thou shalt not steal."
Exod. 20:15
Consider this commandment:
1. In relation to the question of capital and labor.

2. In relation to the question of commercial morality.
3. In relation to individual conduct towards God and towards man.

—R. J. Wardell, *A Manual of Sermon Construction*

22. WITH GOD IN THE DARK

"*And the people stood afar off, and Moses drew near unto the thick darkness where God was.*"
Exod. 20:21

The thick darkness—and God! This is the paradox. Take it of:
1. The darkness of history.
2. The dark night of the soul.
3. The darkness of sin.
4. The darkness of death.

—James S. Stewart,
in *Sermons I Should Like To Have Preached*

23. THE DIAMOND

"*And the second row shall be an emerald, a sapphire, and a diamond.*"   Exod. 28:18

Every true Christian is a spiritual jewel, one of God's diamonds.

What are the points of comparison? What is there about a diamond which ought to be characteristic of the follower of Christ?
1. Its hardness.
   A diamond is one of the hardest things in the world.
   a) It will bear a great deal of rough handling without being scratched or damaged at all.
   b) It can make marks that cannot be rubbed out.

2. Its brightness.
   It is the most brilliant of all jewels. There is no light inherent in itself, but it is many-faceted and flashes and sparkles with reflected glory.
3. Its trueness.
   There are such things as counterfeit diamonds. Men can make imitation jewels. But there are two tests by which they can be readily distinguished from the genuine precious stone.
   a) A real diamond cannot be scratched.

W. L. Watkinson wrote: "Many years ago in Brazil a slave found what was supposed to be a diamond of nearly a pound weight. It was presented to the emperor, constantly guarded by soldiers, and was supposed to represent millions of dollars. But an English mineralogist produced a cutting diamond, and scratched the supposed mammoth prize. One scratch was enough. If it had been a real gem, it would not have taken a scratch."

   b) A real diamond shines undimmed under water. When immersed in water, counterfeit diamonds lose their lustre. Genuine diamonds burn as brilliantly as ever.

—Richard Newton

24. SHIFTING RESPONSIBILITY

"*There came out this calf.*"
Exod. 32:24

Aaron was desperately anxious to avoid the suspicion of complicity in the production of the Golden Calf. Watch him trying to shift the

21

responsibility from his shoulders.

1. He blames chance.
"There came out this calf." A famous preacher called this the "automatic calf."
2. He blames nature.
"I cast it into the fire."
As if it were not his fault but nature's. He says nothing about the mold that he had made; nothing about the graving tool that he used. Exod. 32:4. Nature has done it.
3. He blamed society.
"[They] gathered themselves together unto Aaron."
Exod. 34:1
He should have blamed himself!

—W. L. Watkinson,
The Bane and the Antidote
(adapted)

25. THE FACE OF GOD

"My presence [literally, my face] shall go with thee." Exod. 33:14

When Thomas Carlyle was a little boy, he was once out walking with his father. They came to a stream in full flood, across which was only a narrow plank bridge. The small Thomas was terrified, and stood immovable. His father took him up in his arms and carried him across, but he carried him face downwards so that he was looking at the foaming, angry waters. Though he knew his father would not let him go, he was nevertheless shivering with fear. Afterwards, recalling the incident, he said: "Had it been my mother, she would have given me her face to look at!"

—G. T. Bellhouse

God gives us his face to look at!
Several facts about a face:

1. A face indicates identity.
2. A face displays emotion.
3. A face expresses character.
4. A face shows direction.

26. GLIMPSES OF GOD

"And he said, I beseech thee, show me thy glory." Exod. 33:18 ff.

1. The request.
"I beseech thee."
2. The response.
"I will make all my goodness pass before thee."
Exod. 33:19
3. The realization.
"The Lord passed by before him." Exod. 34:6
4. The result.
"Moses . . . worshipped."
Exod. 34:8

—B. G. Newton,
Glimpses of God

LEVITICUS

27. THE UNDYING FLAME

"The fire shall ever be burning upon the altar; it shall never go out."

Lev. 6:13

Think of:
1. The flame of moral indignation.
2. The flame of personal consecration.
3. The flame of pentecostal inspiration.

NUMBERS

28. GIANTS AND GRASSHOPPERS

"And there we saw the giants, the sons of Anak, which come of the giants: and we were in our own sight as grasshoppers, and so we were in their sight." Num. 13:33

In the battle of life, it is all-important to get one's "sights" right.

1. Depreciative self-estimate. "Our own sight."
2. The low opinion of others. "Their sight."
3. What God thinks of us. God's sight.

—David H. C. Read, *Sons of Anak*

29. SIN FINDING OUT

"Be sure your sin will find you out." Num. 32:23

There are different ways in which sin finds out the sinner. Consider four of them:

1. By remorse of conscience.
2. By the operation of moral law.
3. By the divine discipline of life.
4. By the awful revelations of the Day of Judgment.

—William Garden Blaikie, *For the Work of the Ministry* (adapted)

DEUTERONOMY

30. THE PARABLE OF THE EAGLE'S NEST

"As the eagle. . . . so the Lord." Deut. 32:11

What does it reveal?

1. It is a revelation of the God who builds.
2. It is a revelation of the God who breaks.
3. It is a revelation of the God who broods.
4. It is a revelation of the God who bears.

—F. W. Boreham, *The Three Half-moons*

31. THE AQUILINE LIFE

"As an eagle stirreth up her nest." Deut. 32:11

"Thy youth is renewed like the eagle's." Ps. 103:5
"They shall mount up with wings as eagles." Isa. 40:31

Many may recall the magnificent description of the eagle which we owe to the poet Tennyson:

He clasps the crag with hookèd hands;
Close to the sun in lonely lands,
Ring'd with the azure world, he stands.

The wrinkled sea beneath him crawls;
He watches from his mountain walls,
And like a thunderbolt he falls.

The Bible compares the man of God to an eagle. It says that the man is:

1. Stirred up like the eagle. "As an eagle stirreth up."

23

2. Toned up like the eagle. "Renewed like the eagle's."

3. Mounting up like the eagle. "Mount up . . . as eagles."

JOSHUA

32. SPRINGS OF WATER

"Thou hast given me a south land; give me also springs of water."
Josh. 15:19

1. Springs of water mean abundance.
2. Springs of water mean beauty.
3. Springs of water mean music.

—Douglas M. Joss, *Springs of Water*

33. CHOOSE

"Choose you this day whom ye will serve." Josh. 24:15

These words have a military ring. They are the words of the soldier— short, sharp, decisive.

Their import will appear if we consider that:

1. The service of God is a matter of choice.
"Choose you."
2. The choice of God is a matter of service.
"Whom ye will serve."
3. Neither the choice nor the service admits any delay.
"This day."

—M. R. Drury,
in *Snappy Sermon Starters*

RUTH

34. LOYALTY TO GOD IN HUMAN RELATIONS

"Entreat me not to leave thee, or to return from following after thee: for whither thou goest, I will go; and where thou lodgest, I will lodge: thy people shall be my people, and thy God my God."
Ruth 1:16

Loyalty here means love in everyday action:

1. In loving a mother-in-law.
Ruth 1
2. In dealing with men.
Ruth 2
3. In finding a mate.
Ruth 3
4. In making a home.
Ruth 4

—Andrew W. Blackwood,
Expository Preaching for Today

24

I SAMUEL

35. THREE READINGS OF LIFE'S RIDDLE

"It was . . . chance."
I Sam. 6:9

As the solution of the problem of human existence:

1. Some see luck.
2. Some see law.
3. Some see love.

—W. L. Stephen,
A Great Nation

36. THE SWORD INCOMPARABLE

"And David said unto Abimelech, And is there not here under thine hand spear or sword? for I have neither brought my sword nor my weapons with me, because the king's business required haste. And the priest said, The sword of Go- liath *the Philistine, whom thou slewest in the valley of Elah, behold, it is here, wrapped in a cloth behind the ephod: if thou wilt take that, take it; for there is none other save that here. And David said, There is none like that; give it me."*
I Sam. 21:8-9

1. There was none like it because of past associations.
   Goliath's sword!
2. There was none like it because of its present consecration.
   "Wrapped in a cloth behind the ephod."
3. There was none like it for personal appropriation.
   "Give it me."

Note: Apply all this to the "sword of the Spirit, which is the word of God." Eph. 6:17

II SAMUEL

37. DEAR FOR HIS SAKE

"Is there yet any that is left of the house of Saul, that I may show him kindness for Jonathan's sake?"
II Sam. 9:1

1. Some are not dear at all.
2. Some are dear for their own sake.
3. Some are dear for the sake of Another.
   Such are we at the Table of the Lord.

38. THE SUPREME VISION

"Now therefore let me see the king's face." II Sam. 14:32

These are fair words on foul lips. It was the faithless Absalom who used them. But the words may be employed to express the purest, holiest longings of which our hearts are capable.

"Let me see the king's face." Is not this:

1. The inspiration of worship?
2. The succor in temptation?
3. The spur to service?
4. The solace for suffering?
5. The endless bliss of heaven?

—H. O. Mackey,
Miniature Sermons

25

39. HOMESICK

"And David longed, and said, Oh that one would give me drink of the water of the well of Bethlehem, which is by the gate!"

II Sam. 23:15

The natural heart craves three homes:

1. A domestic home.
2. A church home.
3. An eternal home.

—Hugh Latimer Elderdice, in *Snappy Sermon Starters*

40. WANTING THE IMPOSSIBLE

"Oh that one would give me drink of the water of the well of Bethlehem, which is by the gate!"

II Sam. 23:15

Note here:

1. The craving that was intolerable.
   The longing that swept over David was more than one of mere physical thirst. That glimpse of Bethlehem, lying in the fold of the hills, had brought back a sudden wave of memories.
2. The circumstances that seemed insurmountable.
   The road to the well was blocked and barred against him.
3. The consecration that was inevitable.
   When the gift of water was put into David's hands, what did he do with it? He poured it out as an offering to God.

—George B. Duncan, *Wanting the Impossible*

I KINGS

41. ALONE AGAINST THE WORLD

"I, even I only, remain a prophet of the Lord" I Kings 18:22
"They all forsook him [Jesus], and fled." Mark 14:50
"At my first answer no man stood with me, but all men forsook me." II Tim. 4:16

More than once in human history it has happened that one man has found himself alone against the world. Athanasius, the champion of orthodoxy in the ancient church, found himself in that position. So did Luther the Protestant reformer, and Galileo the pioneer of astronomical science.

Think of three who stood alone of whom the Bible tells.

1. Alone against the world for pure religion's preservation.
   Elijah before Ahab and Jezebel.
2. Alone against the world for that world's salvation.
   Christ before Pilate.
3. Alone against the world as a witness to revelation.
   Paul before Nero.

II KINGS

42. DIGGING DITCHES

"Thus saith the Lord, Make this valley full of ditches."
II Kings 3:16

What are the ditches that God can and does fill?

1. The ditch of a great desire.
2. The ditch of an expectant faith.
3. The ditch of a devoted service.

—A. Lindsay Glegg, *Walking on Two Feet*

43. MAKING ROOM FOR THE PROPHET

(An Ordination or Induction Sermon)
"Let us make a little chamber, I pray thee, on the wall; and let us set for him [the prophet Elisha] there a bed, and a table, and a stool, and a candlestick: and it shall be, when he cometh to us, that he shall turn in thither."
II Kings 4:10

This charming old-world narrative is, in a sense, as modern as today's newspaper. It tells of a welcome being extended to a prophet, and it is for precisely the same purpose that we are assembled now.

There are four thoughts suggested by the story which it may be for our profit to study for a little.

1. If we want the prophet to stay with us, we shall have to give him an *invitation*.
"She constrained him to eat bread." II Kings 4:8

2. If we want the prophet to stay with us, we shall have to provide him with *accommodation*.
"Let us make a little chamber, I pray thee, on the wall."
II Kings 4:10

3. If we want the prophet to stay with us, we shall not lack *compensation*.
"What is to be done for thee?" II Kings 4:13

4. If we want the prophet to stay with us, we shall experience *resuscitation*.
"The flesh of the child waxed warm." II Kings 4:34

44. IT IS WELL

"Is it well with the child? And she answered, It is well."
II Kings 4:26

1. It is well with those who, being in Christ, are gone to God.
"They dwell in his presence who hath redeemed them, where there is fullness of joy and pleasure for evermore."

2. It is well also with those who are in Christ, though not gone to God.
"The kingdom of God is within you; you feel it. This is a kingdom of righteousness, and peace, and joy in the Holy Ghost."

3. It is well with those who truly desire to be in Christ, that they may go to God.
"He will be found of them that diligently seek him."

27

4. It is well with those who neither desire to be in Christ nor to go to God. "It is well for them that they are not in hell, that the day of grace is not utterly past."

—William Grimshaw

45. UNSEEN ENVIRONMENT

"Lord, I pray thee, open his eyes, that he may see."

II Kings 6:17

Had there been an oculist in Dothan, he would probably have pronounced perfect the eyesight of Elisha's servant. Yet when the servant came to Elisha, crying: "Alas, my master, how shall we do?" the prophet prayed: "Lord, open his eyes, that he may see!" He had been blind to his unseen environment.

Observe that:

1. In the world around us there is the presence and power of a living God, and until we see that presence, we are blind.
2. There are circumstances in which blindness is a blessing. Our ignorance of the future is, on the whole, a mercy. But I am not pleading for vision for tomorrow. I am pleading for the recognition of the divine today.
3. What is the moral value of this unseen environment? It lifts us above circumstances. Did you ever hold in your hand one of those puzzle-cards on which there is something clearly and plainly drawn, and

some face or figure in the lines that is not evident? Here is the garden: find the gardener, for example. And we study the card, hold it at all angles, turn it round and back again, yet for the life of us we cannot see the face. Then, in an instant, there it is! And now we can see nothing else; and we hand it on and wonder how our neighbor can possibly escape detecting what is so plain to us.

—George H. Morrison, Sunrise (adapted)

46. THE SIN OF LOW EXPECTATIONS

"Elisha said, Shoot. . . . And he smote thrice, and stayed. And the man of God was wroth with him, and said, Thou shouldest have smitten five or six times."

II Kings 13:17-19

Notice that:

1. To cherish low expectations is to wrong one's self.
2. To cherish low expectations is to injure others.
3. To cherish low expectations is to limit God.

—Norman McLeod Caie, The Secret of a Warm Heart

47. THE REDISCOVERY OF A LOST BIBLE

"And Hilkiah the high priest said unto Shaphan the scribe, I have found the book of the law in the house of the Lord. And Hilkiah gave the book to Shaphan, and he read it." II Kings 22:8

1. How the Bible may be lost!
   Never through trial and persecution; always through neglect.
2. Where it may be lost!
   In the house of God as well as in the home.
3. How the Bible may be rediscovered!
   a) By seeming accident.
   b) of set purpose through scholarly investigation.

c) by each of us through deliberate and intelligent study.
4. The effect of rediscovery of the Bible.
   Compare the effect on Josiah and his times. See II Kings 22 and 23.

—James Dinwoodie,
*One Hundred Illustrated
Sermon Outlines and Texts*

I CHRONICLES

48. THE PRAYER OF JABEZ

"Oh, that thou wouldest bless me indeed, and enlarge my coast, and that thine hand might be with me, and that thou wouldest keep me from evil, that it may not grieve me." I Chron. 4:10

1. It is a prayer for personal benediction.
   "Oh, that thou wouldest bless me indeed."
2. It is a prayer for practical extension.
   "And enlarge my coast."
3. It is a prayer for providential direction.
   "That thine hand might be with me."
4. It is a prayer for perpetual protection.
   "And that thou wouldest keep me from evil, that it may not grieve me."

—A. Skevington Wood, *Heralds
of the Gospel*

49. UNDER TENSION

"And David said unto Gad, I am in a great strait: let me fall now into the hand of the Lord; for very great are his mercies: but let me not fall into the hand of man."

I Chron. 21:13

Jesus said: *"I have a baptism to be baptized with; and how am I straitened till it be accomplished!"*
Luke 12:50

"I am in a strait betwixt the two, having a desire to depart, and to be with Christ; which is far better: nevertheless to abide in the flesh is more needful for you."
Phil. 1:23

Here we see:
1. David in a strait between God and man.
2. Christ in a strait between present and future.
3. Paul in a strait between life and death.

II CHRONICLES

50. THE VICTORY OF FAITH

"The children of Judah prevailed, because they relied upon the Lord God of their fathers."
II Chron. 13:18

1. Here we have a pattern worth copying.
2. Here we have a promise worth trusting.
   The men of Judah remembered the promise of the Lord God of their fathers to give "the kingdom over Israel to David for ever."
3. Here we have a prospect worth cherishing.
   The prospect which steeled the hearts of the children of Israel in the day of battle was that of certain victory. It could not be otherwise. "Behold," cried Abijah, "God himself is with us for our captain."

—G. N. M. Collins, in *Monthly Record* of Free Church of Scotland, October, 1963

51. THE EYES OF GOD

"The eyes of the Lord run to and fro throughout the whole earth, to show himself strong in the behalf of them whose heart is perfect toward him." II Chron. 16:9

This is a strikingly suggestive text, appealing strongly to the imagination. Reading its description of the eyes of the Lord running to and fro in the earth, one is irresistibly reminded of the blazing headlights of a powerful car, bowling at night along a great highway, blasting the darkness with beams!

Incidentally, notice how the verse recalls the long Latin words in which historic theology speaks of the attributes of God.

1. "The eyes of the Lord."
   Omniscience.
2. "Run to and fro throughout the whole earth."
   Omnipresence.
3. "To show himself strong."
   Omnipotence.
4. "In the behalf of them whose heart is perfect toward him."
   Benevolence.

ESTHER

52. NOT AFRAID OF SACKCLOTH

"None might enter into the king's gate clothed with sackcloth."
Esth. 4:2

There are three ways in which we may deal with the harder things of life. Let us consider them each in turn.

1. The way of escapism.
   We may follow the example of this eastern king, close our eyes and ears, and say that we will not look upon the things that affright and affront us.

2. The way of Stoicism.
We may look willingly or unwillingly at the facts of life without any hope in Christ.
3. The way of Christian realism. We may face the problems and agonies of life without flinching, without fear, as possessors of the Christian hope.

—W. Robertson Nicoll,
The Lamp of Sacrifice (adapted)

JOB

53. THE SCHOOL OF THE BEASTS

"Ask now the beasts, and they shall teach thee." Job 12:7
What have the beasts to teach us?
For instance:

1. The ox.
"The ox knoweth his owner"
Isa. 1:3
The lesson to be learned is that we should know God.
2. The ass.
"Doth the wild ass bray when he hath grass?" Job 6:5
The lesson to be learned is that we should gratefully accept God's provision for us.
3. The serpent.
"Be ye . . . wise as serpents"
Matt. 10:16
The lesson to be learned is that we also should be tactful and diplomatic in our dealings with others.

54. SUCCESSFUL SIN

"The vintage of the wicked."
Job 24:6

The transgression of the law is sometimes visited by an immediate punishment. This is not, however, always the case. So often the sinner seems to escape and his sin appears to be successful.
But consider:

1. The blinding power of successful sin.
   a) It obscures our highest beliefs.
   b) It confuses our moral sense.
2. The beguiling power of successful sin.
In South America a phosphorescent spider is found that attracts and dupes its prey by successive flashes of light. The moth is apparently dazed, and with the emission of each gleam it creeps closer to the transfigured assassin. This is a parable of the process of sin.
3. The torturing power of successful sin.
How vividly Nathaniel Hawthorne depicts this in *The Scarlet Letter!*
4. The blighting power of successful sin.

—W. L. Watkinson,
The Supreme Conquest

55. SONGS IN THE NIGHT

"God my maker, who giveth songs in the night." Job 35:10

31

1. Who is the author of these songs in the night?
God himself.
2. What is the matter contained in these songs in the night?
The day that is past or the day to come.
3. What are the excellences of these songs in the night?
They are hearty and show faith and love.
4. What is the use of songs in the night?
To cheer one's self and encourage others.

—Charles Haddon Spurgeon

56. THE TREASURES OF THE SNOW

"Hast thou entered into the treasures of the snow?"

Job 38:22

Consider:

1. How strong the snow is!
It can block roads and railway lines. It can stop mighty locomotives. Napoleon was halted on his path to world empire by the might of the snowflakes!

2. How useful the snow is!
It warms and waters the earth: it is like a white blanket keeping nature warm.
3. How beautiful the snow is!
It can transform the dingiest and most dismal scene and make it sparkle like a view of fairyland.
4. How silent the snow is!
Thousands of tons of it can fall in the night and no one will be aware of its descent until the light reveals its presence in the morning.
5. How challenging the snow is!
Other things may look white until brought into revealing comparison with the snow: then how dull and soiled they seem! Think of F. B. Meyer visiting a woman on washday and complimenting her on the brightness of the clothes hanging on the line. Then snow fell. At once the whiteness lost its luster. The clothes appeared positively dirty beside the dazzling brilliance of the snow.

PSALMS 1–46

57. TREES OF THE LORD

"He shall be like a tree planted by the rivers of water, that bringeth forth his fruit in his season."

Ps. 1:3

Here we have a picture of:

1. Fixity.
"Planted."
2. Virility.
"By rivers of water."

3. Fertility.
"That bringeth forth."
4. Utility.
"His fruit."
5. Reliability.
"In his season."

58. TREES OF THE LORD

"He shall be like a tree planted by the rivers of water." Ps. 1:3

Here is a picture of the good man (a) as he shall be; (b) as he thirsts to be; and (c) as in a measure he is.

1. Such a tree is the product of skillful husbandry.
   It is not a wild tree—"planted." It is in a valley. Pride would choose the hilltop. It is by a river—perennial, unfailing supply of spiritual needs.
2. Such a tree is an emblem of stability.
3. Such a tree is a representative of vitality.
4. Such a tree is a picture of beauty.
5. Such a tree is a symbol of utility.

—*Stems and Twigs*

59. THE LIFE OF LOVE

(A Pictorial Exposition of Ps. 23)

1. A morning meal in the meadows.
   "He maketh me to lie down in green pastures." Ps. 23:2
2. A midday drink from the well.
   "He leadeth me beside the still waters." Ps. 23:2
3. A noontide rest in the shade.
   "He restoreth my soul."
   Ps. 23:3
4. An afternoon climb on the paths.
   "He leadeth me in the paths of righteousness for his name's sake." Ps. 23:3
5. Adventures in the shadowed glen.
   "Yea, though I walk through the valley of the shadow of death, I will fear no evil."
   Ps. 23:4

6. Supper on the darkening wold.
   "Thou preparest a table before me." Ps. 23:4
7. Twilight at the sheepfold door.
   "Thou anointest my head with oil; my cup runneth over." Ps. 23:4
8. Night within the gates.
   "Surely goodness and mercy shall follow me all the days of my life." Ps. 23:6
9. Foregleams of the heavenly dawn.
   "And I will dwell in the house of the Lord for ever."
   Ps. 23:6

—J. D. Freeman,
Life on the Uplands

60. THE UPLIFTED GATES

"Lift up your heads, O ye gates."
Ps. 24:7

"Ancient gates did not open on hinges, but were drawn up and down by weights and pulleys. The top seems to have been ornamented with the resemblance of a human head."

Hence, "lift up your heads, O ye gates!"

See how these words can be applied:

1. To the first Advent when the gates of human history were lifted up to let in the King of Glory.
2. To the Atonement when the gates of Hades were lifted up to let Christ in.
   "By which [the Spirit] also he went and preached unto the spirits in prison."
   I Pet. 3:19

33

3. To the Ascension when the gates of heaven were lifted up to let Christ in.
4. To the announcement of the gospel when the gates of human hearts are lifted up to let Christ in.
5. To the Second Advent when again the gates of human history will be lifted up to let in the King of Glory.

61. SPIRITUAL PHONETICS

"Be not silent unto me: lest if thou be silent unto me, I become like them that go down into the pit."
Ps. 28:1
"After the fire a still small voice."
I Kings 19:12
"And the Word was made flesh, and dwelt among us." John 1:14
"And suddenly there came a sound from heaven." Acts 2:2

It cannot honestly be claimed that this is a sound age, but neither can it be denied that it is an age of sound. The times may be "phoney" in one sense. They are also "phoney" in another. Telephones, gramophones, microphones, and so forth, fill our days with a multitude of sounds.

But what about the sound from heaven? What about spiritual electronics?

The texts have in common a connection with this subject. To read them is like turning the knob on a tape recorder from zero upwards.

1. Silence.
"Be not silent unto me: lest, if thou be silent unto me, I

34

become like them that go down into the pit."
Ps. 28:1
Note:
a) Sometimes God is silent to us because we are not ready for the revelation.
b) Sometimes God is silent to us because we are not willing for the revelation.
c) Sometimes God is silent to us because we are not worthy of the revelation.
"O Lord," prayed Luther, "smite us, but be not silent unto us."
2. The still small voice.

"Dog trainers sometimes use a silent dog whistle. It is an adaptation of a device of Francis Galton, the anthropologist, and is probably older than he. It is based on the fact that dogs can hear higher notes than human beings, and Galton is said to have amused himself by startling all the little dogs in the park by a sound their owners did not hear." —W. E. Sangster

A wag has defined conscience as "the still small voice which makes us feel still smaller."
3. The Word.
"And the Word was made flesh." John 1:14
They asked John the Baptist: "Who are you? Who are you?" And he replied: "I am a voice, but the Word is coming after me." The voice passes; the Word remains.

4. The echo.
"And suddenly there came a sound from heaven."

Acts 2:2

That word "echo" is an exact transcription of the Greek for "sound." This sound was an echo. The Word had been uttered on earth, and now at Pentecost the echo was coming back from heaven.

62. WE WILL REMEMBER THEM

(An Armistice Day Sermon)
"*Forgotten as a dead man out of mind.*" Ps. 31:12

It is only natural for us to forget the dead. However much we love and revere them, we cannot hold them forever in our recollection. Life moves us on. And eventually the memory of those of our acquaintance who have passed away tends to vanish from our minds as their forms have disappeared from our sight.

Despite this, there are some whom it is our bounden duty to remember. Such are those who, in battle, have given their lives for us. That is why it is good to keep such a day as this in green remembrance.

But just how are we to call to mind those whom we are obligated to remember?

We should:

1. Remember them with gratitude.
Recall the stately lines of Laurence Binyon in his poem, "For the Fallen":

They shall not grow old,
as we that are left grow old:
Age shall not weary them
nor the years condemn.
At the going down of the sun
and in the morning
We will remember them.

2. Remember with pride.
3. Remember with regret.
At its best and bravest, war is a bloody business, "the sum of all the villainies."

Remember most of all him who gave his life for us as no soldier ever could!

63. OUR TIMES— HIS HAND

"*My times are in thy hand.*"
Ps. 31:15

Observe that our times are in God's hands:

1. In the sense that he determined the date of our birth on earth.
2. In the sense that he desires to direct our daily doings.
3. In the sense that he has decided the date of our departure from the world.

64. SPIRITUAL THERAPEUTICS

"*Rest in the Lord, and wait patiently for him.*" Ps. 37:7

Rest is a cardinal principle in natural therapeutics. So also is it in the spiritual.

I have three things to say:

1. Remember God.
2. Rely on God.
3. Rest in God.

—Bernard J. Snell,
The Virtue of Gladness

65. THE AUTOBIOGRAPHY OF A CHRISTIAN

"He brought me up also out of an horrible pit, out of the miry clay, and set my feet upon a rock, and established my goings. And he hath put a new song in my mouth, even praise unto our God: many shall see it, and fear, and shall trust in the Lord." Ps. 40:2, 3

Here is the autobiography of a Christian. There are five chapters to the story. Their headings are as follows:

1. Brought up.
   "He brought me up also out of an horrible pit."
2. Set up.
   "[He] set my feet upon a rock."
3. Held up.
   "And established my goings."
4. Tuned up.
   "He hath put a new song in my mouth, even praise unto our God."
5. Caught up.
   For this I have gone to the end of the psalm, and taken a verse out of its context: "Make no tarrying, O my God."

—A. Lindsay Glegg,
Life With a Capital "L"

66. THE SEARCH FOR THE DIVINE

"Where is thy God?" Ps. 42:3

Here are seven answers to that question:

1. He is above us.
   "The Lord your God, he is God in heaven above."
   Josh. 2:11

2. He is around us.
   "As the mountains are round about Jerusalem, so the Lord is round about his people."
   Ps. 125:2
3. He is before us.
   "The Lord went before them." Exod. 13:21
4. He is behind us.
   "The glory of the Lord shall be thy rearward." Isa. 58:8
5. He is beneath us.
   "Underneath are the everlasting arms." Deut. 33:27
6. He is with us.
   "I am with thee . . . I am thy God." Isa. 41:10
7. He is in us.
   "Christ in you, the hope of glory." Col. 1:27

—Robert L. Layfield,
in *Snappy Sermon Starters*

67. CHRIST'S THREE ANOINTINGS

"God, thy God, hath anointed thee with the oil of gladness above thy fellows." Ps. 45:7
"He hath anointed me to preach." Luke 4:18
"God anointed Jesus of Nazareth with the Holy Ghost and with power: who went about doing good." Acts 10:38
"She is come aforehand to anoint My body to the burying." Mark 14:8

Christ was:

1. Anointed to sovereignty.
2. Anointed to service.
   a) By word. Luke 4:18
   b) By works. Acts 10:38
3. Anointed to suffering.

PSALMS 50–148

68. THE SILENCE OF GOD

"And I kept silence." Ps. 50:21

Our theme is the silence of God in face of human sin.

"These things hast thou done, and I kept silence."

Consider:

1. God's silence as the effect of his wonderful patience.
2. God's silence which is a judicial infliction.
3. God's silence as a temporary discipline imposed for our good.
4. God's silence as a provisional accommodation to our present incapacity to comprehend.

—Unknown

69. GOD'S HARVEST BOUNTY

(A Harvest-Thanksgiving Sermon)

"Thou preparest them corn." Ps. 65:9

The text teaches that:

1. God keeps his promises. "While the earth remaineth, seedtime and harvest, and cold and heat, and summer and winter, and day and night shall not cease." Gen. 8:22

   There is a story of an old lady who, from year to year, kept a few ears of corn in her home. "I keep them," she explained to an inquirer, "to remind me that God will never break his promise."
2. God brings much out of little.

It may take ten men to harvest what one man has sown.

3. God turns death into life. "Except a corn of wheat fall into the ground and die, it abideth alone: but if it die, it bringeth forth much fruit." John 12:24
4. God causes the harvest to be of the same kind as the seed. "Be not deceived; God is not mocked: for whatsoever a man soweth, that shall he also reap." Gal. 6:7

—H. O. Mackey, *Miniature Sermons*

70. OF ONE MIND IN ONE HOUSE

"He is the God that maketh men to be of one mind in an house." Ps. 68:6, *Book of Common Prayer*

Note:

1. When people live in one house, they had better be of one mind!
2. If this is to be, someone will have to make them so.
3. Only God can do it!

71. MAN'S WRATH PRAISING GOD

"Surely, the wrath of man shall praise thee." Ps. 76:10

Notice how this principle works out in biblical history:

1. Consider what happened when Pharaoh issued an edict that all Hebrew children should be slain—Moses was

adopted by Pharaoh's own daughter!

2. Consider how Goliath gave God a chance to reveal his power.
3. Consider Darius' decree . . . Daniel's refusal . . . Darius' new decree.
4. Consider how man's wrath crucified Jesus, but millions now glory in the cross.
5. Consider how, as a result of the persecution of the primitive church, Christianity was spread abroad.
6. Consider how when Paul was put in prison, his very guards were converted, and how the great apostle went to the outposts of the Roman Empire at the emperor's expense as a Christian evangelist.

—Paul E. Holdcraft,
Snappy Sermon Starters

72. GOD'S WAY

"Thy way, O God, is in the sanctuary." Ps. 77:13

1. God's way of convincing is in the sanctuary.
2. God's way of converting is in the sanctuary.
3. God's way of comforting is in the sanctuary.
4. God's way of challenging is in the sanctuary.

—W. Price,
Sketches of Sermons

73. INEXCUSABLE

"The children of Ephraim, being armed, and carrying bows, turned back in the day of battle."
Ps. 78:9

1. Their ancestry made them inexcusable.
"The tribe of Ephraim was so important as often to give its name to the kingdom of Israel:"—Alexander Maclaren
2. Their panoply made them inexcusable.
"Being armed, and carrying bows."
3. Their opportunity made them inexcusable.
"In the day of battle."
Consider these things in relation to the Christian conflict.

74. OPEN-MOUTHED

"Open thy mouth wide, and I will fill it." Ps. 81:10

G. K. Chesterton is often quoted as saying that the real reason for opening the mind, like that for opening the mouth, is—to close it again on something solid! In our text "something solid" is promised to the one who opens his mouth wide.

We can take the words in three ways.

1. Literally.

"The figure in our text is a little picture taken from nature. We have often seen a brood of young birds in the nest in early spring: half-a-dozen tiny, helpless things, conscious of nothing but their own wants, unable to provide for themselves, entirely dependent on parental care. They hear the twitter of the parent bird on the neighbouring branch, and they know what it means. It means that a meal is about to be served and, full of expectation, lifting up their little heads, with beaks wide open, they prepare to receive it. Alighting on the edge of the nest, the parent bird gives to each its food amid shrill cries of delight."

2. Spiritually.

If every hunger has its food and every thirst its drink, shall man's spiritual nature be an exception? God supplies the food, but he does not prize our jaws open and cram it down. He tells us to open our mouths. That is all we have to do, but we have to do it. And we can do it by prayer, by Bible study and by meditation.

3. Homiletically.

The promise holds good in the ministry too. But it had better not be in the pulpit that we begin to open our mouths wide: The result may be that they will be filled with nothing but hot air!

75. LONGING FOR GOD

"My heart and my flesh crieth out for the living God."   Ps. 84:2

Three things conspire to make us long for the living God.

They are:

1. The sense of incompleteness.
2. The sense of sinfulness.
3. The sense of meaninglessness.

76. THE SUN

"The Lord God is a sun."

Ps. 84:11

It is told of William Joseph Turner, the great English artist, that when he was dying, someone drew up the blind of a window of the room in which he lay. The painter, taking a last look at the sun, cried: "That is my god!"

To him the sun was a god: to the Christian God is a sun.

Observe that:

1. God is like the sun in his controlling centrality.
2. God is like the sun in his vitalizing activity.
3. God is like the sun in his absolute indispensability.

In the frozen wastes of the north where in winter the sun never shines, when spring comes, the people put on their best clothes and climb to the summits of the hills to see the sun return. And when the first rim of red appears on the horizon, they grow almost hysterical with delight, exclaiming: "The sun! The sun! The sun has come back to us!"

77. AS A TALE THAT IS TOLD

"We spend our years as a tale that is told."   Ps. 90:9

Note that:

1. Some tales are false and others are true.
2. Some tales are quiet and unexciting, others are full of movement and incident.
3. Some are tales of joy and others are tales of sorrow.
4. Some are tales that close on a note of tragedy, and others that end amid the jubilations of victory.

—Alexander Stewart,
Shoes for the Road

39

78. THE INVESTMENT OF THE YEARS

"We spend our years as a tale."
Ps. 90:9

1. How the years may be spent:
   a) There are those who spend life as a miser spends.
   b) There are those who spend life like a spendthrift.
   c) There is the Christian way of spending the years.
2. The tale to be told.
   There are three tales which life may tell.
   a) To some, life must be a love story.
   b) Others will want to write an adventure story with their lives.
   c) There is still another story, and it is greater than these. It is the story of the gospel.

—Unknown

79. THE PALM

"The righteous shall flourish like the palm tree." Ps. 92:12

There is in nature a correspondence between living men and living things, and both are the product of one great mind.

The correspondence in our text is between a palm tree and a righteous man.

Let us notice a few points of similarity.

1. Both are subject to a hidden power.
   The life is within, and consequently the growth must begin there. Only inanimate things grow from without.
2. Both grow upward.
   As the plant attracts to itself all it can assimilate, so the believer is constantly drawing to himself all that will strengthen him in his spiritual life and enable him to mount still higher in thought, word, and deed.
3. Both grow downward.
   The righteous stand fast by being firmly rooted and grounded in the faith.
4. Both grow steadily.
   The palm grows steadily whether the season be wet or dry. Steady growth in the Christian requires patience and perseverance.
5. Both grow in fruitfulness.
   Perfection in the vegetable world is not attained until that which has come from a seed reproduces many similar seeds. Fruitfulness in the righteous man is dual. First, there is the fruit he bears in his own life, and second, there is the fruit he bears in the lives of others.
6. Both are evergreen.
   The palm is perennially in leaf. Its foliage never falls. So the righteous is spiritually evergreen.

—John Mitchell,
Stones for Sermon Builders

80. GOD AND THE GODS

"All the gods of the nations are idols, but the Lord made the heavens." Ps. 96:5

I was thinking the other day about the gods of antiquity—Ahura Mazda of ancient Persia, Osiris of

Egypt, Zeus of Greece, Jove of Rome, and Thor of the Teutonic peoples.

Rapidly, I passed them all in mental review, and then I reflected that every one of them has gone, that nobody believes in them anymore. Advancing civilization has left them behind. Higher cultures have dismissed them as mere figments of the primitive imagination. Progress has relegated them to the scrapheap of the past, the oblivion of the obsolete. To the modern age they are almost unknown, and in any case totally irrelevant.

Thereupon the chilling thought struck me: "What if God himself were to be left behind? What if he were to become outmoded? What if Jehovah were to become as dèmodé as Jupiter or Jove? What if God should share the fate of the gods?"

Then I recalled this text, and I saw at once that, while the gods men make may pass away, the God who made men can never pass away.

Think of God as the Maker.

1. "Let us make."
   Gen. 1:26. That is the divine resolution to create.
2. "I will make."
   Matt. 4:19. That is the divine promise to recreate.
3. "Behold, I make."
   Rev. 21:5. That is the divine announcement that the new creation is complete.

81. DIVINE DEALINGS

George Eliot in her novel of that name makes Silas Marner say,

"There's dealin's with us—there's dealin's!"

There certainly are! Let us turn to the Bible and note how it describes them.

1. As a father pitieth.
                    Ps. 103:13
2. As a mother comforteth.
                    Isa. 66:13
3. As a hen gathereth.
                    Matt. 23:27
4. As a bridegroom rejoiceth.
                    Isa. 62:5
5. As a refiner sitteth.
                    Mal. 3:3
6. As an eagle fluttereth.
                    Deut. 32:11
7. As a nurse cherisheth.
                    I Thess. 2:7
8. As a shepherd seeketh.
                    Ezek. 34:12

—Paul E. Holdcraft,
Snappy Sermon Starters
(altered)

82. YOUR SOUL UNDER THE SEARCHLIGHT

"O Lord, thou hast searched me, and known me." Ps. 139:1 ff.

Everyone stands in awe before Ps. 139. Here your soul passes under God's searchlight.

1. God knows you just as you are. (vss. 1-6)
   a) everything good he sees and blesses.
   b) everything evil he wishes to remove.
2. God goes with you wherever you go. (vss. 7-12)
3. God has made you what you are. (vss. 13-18)
4. God wants you to battle on his side. (vss. 19-24)

41

Under the searchlight, a man feels his need of the cross.

—Andrew W. Blackwood,
Expository Preaching for Today

83. THE GOD OF THE YEARS

(A New Year Sermon)

"Thou hast beset me behind and before, and laid thine hand upon me." Ps. 139:5

What a word from the Lord for these opening days of the New Year!

1. God is behind me.
   Taking care of all my yesterdays.
2. God is before me.
   Taking care of all my tomorrows.
3. God is beside me.
   Taking care of today.

—David Hood in *The Christian*,
January 1, 1965

84. YOUTH AND AGE

"Both young men, and maidens; old men, and children; let them praise the name of the Lord." Ps. 148:12, 13

The young have special needs of their own which the gospel must recognize if it is to be of any use to them; and the mature or aged, in like manner, have their own special wants, which cannot be met by the provision made for the young, but can only be satisfied by a gospel which understands and sympathizes with them.

Christ is able to meet the needs of both!

1. For the young, he has the gospel of living; for the old, the gospel of dying.
2. For the young, he has the gospel of inspiration; for the old, the gospel of consolation.
3. For the young, he has the gospel of giving; for the old, the gospel of receiving.

—James Stalker, *The Four Men*

PROVERBS

85. ANTS

"Go to the ant, thou sluggard; consider her ways, and be wise." Prov. 6:6

1. Ants teach us what little people can do.
2. Ants teach us a lesson in industry.
3. Ants teach us a lesson in co-operativeness.
4. Ants teach us a lesson in perseverance.

5. Ants teach us a lesson in law and order.

—Paul E. Holdcraft,
Snappy Sermon Starters

86. THE IDEAL WIFE

(Outline for Wedding Speech)

"Whoso findeth a wife findeth a good thing." Prov. 18:22

Someone has said that an ideal wife will be:

1. Slow as a snail.
   Leaving her own house, but not like the snail carrying all she has on her back.
2. Like an echo.
   Obeying what her husband says, but not like the echo having always the last word.
3. Like a public clock.
   Keeping her home with regularity and orderliness, yet not like the public clock talking so loudly that all her neighbors can hear.

ECCLESIASTES

87. THE SUPREMACY OF CHARACTER

"A good name is better than precious ointment." Eccl. 7:1

There are at least three points of resemblance between a good name and precious ointment, which are well worth noting.
1. There is a point of contact in the element of costliness.

He that filches from me my good name
Robs me of that which not enriches him
And makes me poor indeed.
—Shakespeare, Othello, III, iii

2. There is a point of contact in the quality of usefulness.
   Ointment serves many useful purposes. In the East it was used for refreshing and strengthening the body, for consecrating men to high office, for healing the sick, and for embalming the dead.
3. There is a point of contact in the quality of fragrance.
   A good name diffuses itself like a delightful aroma.

—Alexander Stewart,
Shoes for the Road

88. BLUNTNESS

"If the iron be blunt, and he do not whet the edge, then must he put to more strength."
Eccl. 10:10

Men, like tools, become blunted.
1. Mental powers sometimes lose edge.
2. Moral powers become blunted.
3. Blunted powers, like blunted tools, are troublesome to work.
4. Blunted tools will not turn out good workmanship.
5. Blunted powers, like tools, require sharpening.
   How?
   a) Rest and recreation.
   b) Reading.
   c) Good company.
   d) Prayer.

—Evan Thomas,
When Ye Come Together

89. BREAD UPON THE WATERS

"Cast thy bread upon the waters: for thou shalt find it after many days." Eccl. 11:1

43

These words present us with a picture of four things:

1. The casting.
   "Cast thy bread." There was to be a liberal dissemination of the seed upon the floodwaters.

2. The risking.
   "Upon the waters." It looked like this was throwing it away!

3. The finding.
   "Thou shalt find it."

4. The waiting.
   "After many days."

SONG OF SOLOMON

90. THREE STAGES OF LOVE

"My beloved is mine, and I am his." Song of Sol. 2:16
"I am my beloved's, and my beloved is mine." Song of Sol. 6:3
"I am my beloved's, and his desire is toward me." Song of Sol. 7:10

Here we see:

1. Love possessive and possessed.
2. Love possessed and possessive.
3. Love content to be possessed and no longer possessive.

—Robert Lee, *Outlined Bible*

ISAIAH

91. THE NAMES GOD GAVE TO JESUS

"Behold, a virgin shall conceive, and bear a son, and shall call his name Immanuel." Isa. 7:14
"Thou shalt call his name Jesus; for he shall save his people from their sins." Matt. 1:21
"Wherefore God also hath highly exalted him, and given him a name which is above every name." Phil. 2:9

It is the privilege of a father to name his son. What parent is not proud to avail himself of this paternal prerogative?

In our texts we see God, the eternal Father, naming his Son!

1. The name of prophecy.
2. The name of history.
3. The name of eternity.

92. THE WONDERFUL CHRIST

"His name shall be called Wonderful." Isa. 9:6

In his book *The Ecumenical Movement* Norman Goodall writes:

It was my privilege to visit Bishop Berggrav in his house in Oslo not long

44

before his death. I had not seen him for several years and in the meantime he had been seriously ill. "How are you?" I asked. "Well," he replied, "I'm no better and no worse than when we met last." "That means you're still wonderful," I said. "No," he answered in a flash, "only still wondering!"

Jesus has us all wondering. He is the wonderful Christ.

Consider:

1. The wonder of his birth. "God and Man in oneness blending."
2. The wonder of his teaching. "Having never learned" (John 7:15), yet the greatest teacher of all.
3. The wonder of his miracles. A human Jesus, who could be weak and weary, and yet who wrought works of supernatural power.
4. The wonder of his character. In him we see perfectly combined strength and tenderness, authority and appeal, dogmatism and pictoriality.
5. The wonder of his death. Immortal and yet dying for us and for our sins.
6. The wonder of his rising. Only from one point of view is Christ's resurrection a marvel: from another, it was the most natural and inevitable thing conceivable. As George Matheson put it: "It is no miracle that Jesus rose from the dead; it would have been a miracle if He had not risen."

And so we might go on, speaking of the wonders of Christ. Everything about him is wonderful. But to the Christian, the greatest wonder of all is the wonder of the fact that he is our friend.

93. SETTING THE HOUSE IN ORDER

"Set thine house in order."
Isa. 38:1

Few things are more depressing than a disorderly house. One can ignore disorder, more or less successfully, when one finds it out-of-doors—although there too it is unpleasant—but when one has to live with it, that is another matter. To anyone with a domestic conscience, it then becomes an offense, a reproof, a challenge that "may not be denied."

Consider that:

1. The house of the world needs to be set in order.
2. The house of the church needs to be set in order.
3. The house of the individual life needs to be set in order.

Note: Things do not automatically set themselves right: they have to be set right by somebody.

94. THE SYMBOLISM OF TREES

"All flesh is grass." Isa. 40:6

1. Some may never carry in their hands the palm branch of fame.
2. Some may never hold the olive branch of peace.
3. Some may never grasp the evergreen of hope.
4. All must bear the myrtle and cypress of grief and sorrow.

—Robertson of Irvine, Scotland.

45

95. THE ENDURING WORD OF GOD

"The word of our God shall stand for ever." Isa. 40:8

Of God's Word we may note that:

1. It shall stand forever because it is the communication of an eternal Being.
2. It shall stand forever because it is perennially valid and relevant and applicable.
3. It shall stand forever because it is perfect and requires neither diminution nor addition.

96. WHAT IS GOD LIKE?

"To whom then will ye liken God?" Isa. 40:18

We are bid look in three directions for answers to our question.

1. Look at the stars!
   "Lift up your eyes on high, and behold who hath created these." Isa. 40:26
2. Look at history!
   "Why sayest thou, O Jacob, and speakest, O Israel, My way is hid from the Lord?" Isa. 40:27
3. Look at religious experience! "He giveth power to the faint; and to him that hath no might he increaseth strength." Isa. 40:29-31

—H. Maldwyn Hughes, *Faith and Progress*

97. LIVING LIKE THE EAGLE

"They shall mount up with wings as eagles." Isa. 40:31

As much superior as the life of an eagle is to that of a hen should the life of a Christian be to that of him who is not a Christian.

The king of birds is notable for:

1. Length of life.
   "God hath given to us eternal life." I John 5:11
2. Sharpness of sight.
   The eagle can gaze unblinking into the blazing sun. Christ is our Sun of Righteousness. We look to him.
3. Fleetness in flight.
   Swifter on the wing than other birds, the eagle streaks like lightning across the sky. So must we be quick to do the master's will.

98. THE GOD WHO HIDES HIMSELF

"Verily, thou art a God that hidest thyself, O God of Israel, the Saviour." Isa. 45:15

In his meaty book, *The Bondage of the Will*, Martin Luther wrote: "Whenever God hides Himself, and wills not to be known to us, there we have no concern."

That, of course, is true. And yet there is a sense in which God hides himself so that he may be found of us.

Consider how:

1. He hides himself in the universe.

He hides Himself so wondrously,
As if there were no God.
—F. W. Faber

2. He hid himself in Christ.
   "In whom are hid all the treasures of wisdom and knowledge." Col. 2:3

46

3. He hides himself in the church.
4. He hides himself in the heart of the individual believer.

99. SHEPHERDS AND SHEEP

The Bible has much to say about shepherds and sheep. Consider the following three significant references:

1. Shepherdless sheep.
   "All we like sheep have gone astray." Isa. 53:6
2. Sheep led astray by their shepherds.
   "My people hath been lost sheep; their shepherds have caused them to go astray." Jer. 50:6
3. Shepherded sheep.
   "Ye were as sheep going astray; but are now returned unto the Shepherd and Bishop of your souls." I Pet. 2:25

100. LENGTHENING AND STRENGTHENING

"Lengthen thy cords, and strengthen thy stakes." Isa. 54:2

1. "Lengthen thy cords" is the divine appeal to the church.
   a) seeking to win new territories and heathen lands for Jesus Christ.
   b) seeking to bring daily life more and more under the sway of religion.
   c) seeking a wider knowledge of revealed truth.
2. But we must not only lengthen our cords, we must also strengthen our stakes.

There must be an inward confirmation as well as an outward development. Missionary enterprise must go hand in hand with vital personal religion; the quest for new truth must be accompanied by firm adherence to the historic faith. The lengthening without the strengthening can only issue in disaster.
—J. D. Jones, *Elims of Life*

101. THE WATER SELLER'S CRY

"Ho, every one that thirsteth, come ye to the waters, and he that hath no money; come ye, buy, and eat; yea, come, buy wine and milk without money and without price." Isa. 55:1

Notice here:

1. The wares that are offered.
   "Wine and milk."
2. The prices that are charged.
   "Without money and without price."
3. The customers that are served.
   "Every one that thirsteth."

—L. E. Deen, *The Preacher's Workshop*

102. THE TRULY HEALTHY MAN

"Then shall thy light break forth as the morning, and thine health shall spring forth speedily, and thy righteousness shall go before thee; and the glory of the Lord shall be thy rearward." Isa. 58:8

According to the text, true well-being consists of three things:

47

1. Light for the mind.
   "Then shall thy light break forth as the morning."
2. Health for the body.
   "And thine health shall spring forth speedily."
3. Inward goodness of spirit.
   "And thy righteousness shall go before thee."

—D. Marlais Davies,
The Problems of Life

103. THE SEVEN DEADLY SINS OF THE MODERN WORLD

"Your iniquities have separated between you and your God."
Isa. 59:2

1. Pleasure without conscience.
2. Cleverness without character.
3. Science without humanity.
4. Wealth without work.
5. Industry without morality.
6. Politics without principles.
7. Religion without reality.

—E. D. Jarvis,
If Any Man Minister

104. A CROWN FOR GOD

"A crown of glory in the hand of the Lord."   Isa. 62:3

1. Think of the hand of God *gaining the crown.*
2. Think of the hand of God *forming the crown.*
3. Think of the hand of God *holding the crown.*

—David Burns,
Sayings in Symbol

JEREMIAH

105. THE MAKING OF A PROPHET

There would appear to be three clearly marked stages in the developing consciousness of the prophet. They are indicated by the following texts:

1. *Ah, Lord God*—the consciousness of personal inadequacy.
   "Ah, Lord God! behold, I cannot speak: for I am a child."   Jer. 1:6
2. *Speak, Lord*—the consciousness of impending revelation.
   "Then Samuel answered, Speak; for thy servant heareth."   I Sam. 3:10
3. *Thus saith the Lord*—the consciousness of supernatural communication.
   "Thus saith the Lord that created thee, O Jacob, and he that formed thee, O Israel."
   Isa. 43:1

106. LONELINESS

"I sat alone because of thy hand."
Jer. 15:17

There are various kinds of loneliness. Let us think of some of them together.

1. Immoral loneliness.
   The loneliness of sin. "He [Judas] . . . went immediately out; and it was night."
   John 13:30

2. Circumstantial loneliness.
The loneliness of spatial isolation. Elijah "went a day's journey into the wilderness, and came and sat down under a juniper tree."

I Kings 19:4

3. Intellectual loneliness.
The loneliness of mental superiority. "I have yet many things to say unto you, but ye cannot bear them now." John 16:12 This was the loneliness of Galileo, of Newton, of Einstein.

4. Governmental loneliness.
The loneliness of great responsibility. "I am not able to bear all this people alone."

Numbers 11:14

5. Moral loneliness.
The loneliness of those who make a solitary stand for the truth. Athanasius, Savonarola, and Luther knew this. "I sat alone because of thy hand." Jeremiah knew it too.

6. Spiritual loneliness.
The solitude of a soul in private communion with God. "He [Jesus] was alone praying." Luke 9:18

107. DEEP ENGRAVING

"The sin of Judah is written with a pen of iron, and with the point of a diamond; it is graven upon the table of their heart, and upon the horns of your altars."

Jer. 17:1

John Keats, one of the greatest geniuses in English literature, wrote his own epitaph as follows: "Here lies one whose name was writ in water."

Man's sins are not written in water. They are engraved in granite. Consider that they are indelibly inscribed on:

1. The conscience of the sinner himself.
2. The lives of those involved with him in the sin.
3. The records of the eternal God.

But—Christ can erase them!

108. THE POTTER'S WHEEL

"Then I went down to the potter's house; and, behold, he wrought a work on the wheels." Jer. 18:3

It is a familiar scene in Israel—this of a potter at work, fashioning a vessel out of clay. The machinery which he uses is of the simplest kind. He drives a wheel with his foot; and so he sets in motion another wheel—a round, flat disc or plate, of metal or of wood, which lies horizontally before him, and on which he places the clay which is to be used. As the clay revolves, he molds it into shape—he fashions it into the vessel which he wishes to make—by hand or tool.

To the prophet it becomes a parable. He sees God as the Potter, man as the clay, and he observes that God fashions man for his own use.

What does the figure suggest?

1. The power of God.
"Hath not the potter power over the clay?"

Rom. 9:21

There's a divinity
that shapes our ends,
Rough-hew them how we will.
—Shakespeare, Hamlet, V. ii. 10

49

2. The purpose of God.
3. The patience of God.

—John A. Duke,
The Untroubled Heart

109. VISIONS THAT ARE PREACHED

"They speak a vision of their own heart, and not out of the mouth of the Lord." Jer. 23:16

Note that:

1. Some preach a vision of their own hearts.
   They do not attempt to preach the Word, but their own opinions and theories.
2. Some preach a vision of the hearts of others.
   They lay bare the sins and vices of their neighbors.
3. Some preach a vision of the heart of God.
   "For God so loved the world,

that he gave his only begotten Son." John 3:16

—John Mitchell, *Shot and Shell for a Preacher's Gun*

110. FINDING THE WAY

"They shall ask the way to Zion with their faces thitherward.
Jer. 50:5

Here are helps to finding the heavenward way:

1. The map.
   The Bible.
2. The compass.
   Conscience.
3. The signposts.
   Family upbringing, education, gifts, tastes, interests.
4. The inquiries.
   Directions given us by wayfarers whom we ask.

—John Eddison,
Christian Living

LAMENTATIONS

111. YOKES

Think of:

1. The social yoke.
   "It is good for a man that he bear the yoke in his youth."
   Lam. 3:27

2. The spiritual yoke.
   "Take my yoke upon you."
   Matt. 11:29
3. The matrimonial yoke.
   "Be not unequally yoked together with unbelievers.."
   II Cor. 6:14

EZEKIEL

112. STANDING IN THE GAP

"I sought for a man among them, that . . . should stand in the gap before me for the land."
Ezek. 22:30

Men are needed to stand in the gaps created in the Christian church today by:

1. The secession of so many of its members.

2. The removal from its creed of so many historic doctrines.
3. The demission of office by so many of its ministers.

113. MEN OF CONTINU-ANCE

"Sever out men of continuance."
Ezek. 39:14

A good name for Christians!
We ought:

1. To continue in the Word.
   "If ye continue in my word, then are ye my disciples indeed." John 8:31
2. To continue in the faith.
   "Continue in the faith grounded and settled."
   Col. 1:23

3. To continue in well doing.
   "Let us not be weary in well doing." Gal. 6:9

—James Dinwoodie,
Illustrated Sermon Outlines

114. THE RIVER OF SALVATION

"Every thing shall live whither the river cometh." Ezck. 47:9

1. Its source.
   Within the temple.
2. Its course.
   Through the world.
3. Its force.
   "Every thing shall live."

—*Pencil Points*

DANIEL

115. THE FALL OF BELSHAZZAR

"In that night was Belshazzar the king of the Chaldeans slain."
Dan. 5:30

Several truths are enforced by this solemn narrative:

1. God weighs the souls of all men.
2. The sovereign power of conscience.
3. The sheer folly of pride.
4. The exclusion of God brings its own penalty.

—R. J. Smithson,
Night Tragedies of Scripture

116. THE OPEN WINDOW

"His windows being open in his chamber towards Jerusalem."
Dan. 6:10

It was Downing Street, Babylon. And it was one of the most splendid palaces in Babylon. It was the house of the Prime Minister. And the Babylonian slaves within the palace had orders from their master to keep the lattice of that window always open.

We, too, in our modern Babylon need to keep always open the windows of our souls.

1. We need to keep this window

51

open to redeem our lives from drudgery.

2. We need to keep this window open to shed light upon the shadows of life.

3. We need to keep this window open to give us victory over the world.

—John A. Duke,
The Untroubled Heart

117. AT THE WINDOW

"Now when Daniel knew that the writing was signed, he went into his house; and his windows being open in his chamber toward Jerusalem, he kneeled upon his knees three times a day, and prayed, and gave thanks before his God, as he did aforetime." Dan. 6:10

"Bring ye all the tithes into the storehouse, that there may be meat in mine house, and prove me now herewith, saith the Lord of hosts, if I will not open you the windows of heaven . . . that there shall not be room enough to receive it."
Mal. 3:10

Wherever there is a praying Daniel at his window on earth, there is a prayer-answering God at his window in heaven. Human request has as its counterpart divine revival. Human supplication has corresponding to it divine supply. Human appeal has as its consequence divine response. Whenever Daniel is at his window, God is at his!

Daniel at his window in Babylon suggests three things:

1. The vision of the open window.

2. The ventilation of the open window.

Our word "window" is a contraction and corruption of the phrase "wind door." The window of a house was the door at which the wind came in. Its primary purpose was not illumination but ventilation.

3. The victory of the open window.

What a triumph it represented over all the seductions of the surrounding city! Daniel was in Babylon, but he was not looking at Babylon: he was looking away to the city of his fathers, the city of his heart.

HOSEA

118. AS THE DEW

"I will be as the dew unto Israel."
Hos. 14:5

What does this exceedingly beautiful figure convey to us? God comes as the dew.

1. He comes, then, in stillness.
The dew falls very quietly.

There is nothing quite so noiseless as the dew. And it comes only when all is still.

2. He comes, too, in the darkness.
It is not when the sun is shining that the dew falls, but when the sun has gone down.

3. He comes, moreover, in lowliness.
The dew falls heaviest always upon the lowest ground.
—John A. Duke,
The Untroubled Heart

119. GOD AS THE DEW

"I will be as the dew unto Israel."
Hos. 14:5
God here promises to be as the dew to the Jews! Happily, they are not all Jews who are Jews outwardly and not only those who are Jews outwardly are Jews! To every soul that truly seeks him, God comes as the dew.
Observe that:
1. The dew comes gently.
2. The dew comes delightfully.
3. The dew comes seasonably.

—David Burns,
Sayings in Symbol

AMOS

120. AT EASE IN ZION

"Woe to them that are at ease in Zion!" Amos 6:1
1. Some people are not at ease and not in Zion.
They are consciously sinful, but do not know where to find rest.
2. Some people are at ease, but not in Zion.
They are slumbering in sin, unaware of their need of salvation.
3. Some people are at ease in Zion.
They are saved, but they have no desire to serve.
4. Some people are in Zion but not at ease.
They are doing their utmost to promote the city's well-being.

121. A BASKET OF SUMMER FRUIT

(A Harvest Thanksgiving Sermon)

"Behold a basket of summer fruit."
Amos 8:1
1. Looking at a basket of summer fruit, we see opportunity at an end.
The hand of the gatherer has ended the possibility of further growth and mellowness.
2. Looking at a basket of summer fruit, we see husbandry at an end.
The bare tree and the laden basket mark the close of a long and wearying period of work.
3. Looking at a basket of summer fruit, we see dubiety at an end.
Now that the summer is over and the trees stripped, there is no longer any uncertainty as to the result.

—David Burns, *God's Poem*

JONAH

122. IN THE STORM

"There was a mighty tempest in the sea." Jonah 1:4

"There came down a storm of wind on the lake." Luke 8:23

"Not long after there arose . . . a tempestuous wind, called Euroclydon." Acts 27:14

Note here:

1. The man who stirred the storm: Jonah.
2. The Man who stilled the storm: Jesus.
3. The man who stood the storm: Paul.

HABAKKUK

123. THE MIDST OF THE YEARS

"O Lord, revive thy work in the midst of the years." Hab. 3:2

"The midst of the years." A cryptic phrase! Several interpretations of it have been suggested. Think of three of them.

1. Augustine thought that the words applied to the period between the first and second advents of Christ.
2. Calvin was of the opinion that the allusion was to the interval between the captivity of Israel and its restoration.
3. Many see here a reference to the mid-period of human life or of Christian experience.

ZECHARIAH

124. RAIN

"Ask ye . . . rain in the time of the latter rain." Zech. 10:1

Observe that:

1. Rain is cyclical in its incidence.
2. Rain is proportionate in its distribution.

3. Rain is fertilizing in its effects.

125. THE SCARRED CONQUEROR

"What are these wounds in thine hands? Then he shall answer, Those with which I was wounded in the house of my friends." Zech. 13:6

1. The wonder of those wounds. It was threefold:

54

a) where they were received.
b) from whom they were received.
c) that they are retained.

2. The wearer of those wounds.
3. The witness of those wounds.

—George Harper, *One Hundred Sermons in Brief*

MALACHI

126. THREE FUNCTIONS OF FIRE

"For he is like a refiner's fire."
Mal. 3:2

In his great work *Credo ut Intelligam*, Anselm wrote:

The love of God is not a mild benevolence, it is a consuming fire. To those who resist it, it becomes an eternal torment; to those who are willing to face its demands, it becomes a fire that cleanses and purifies. Those whom it has once penetrated, it transforms into itself.

Here three functions of fire are brought before us:

1. Fire consumes.
   "It is a consuming fire."
2. Fire cleanses.
   "A fire that cleanses and purifies."
3. Fire conforms.
   "Those whom it has once penetrated, it transforms into itself."

55

New
Testament

MATTHEW 1–9

127. THE BIRTHDAY OF JESUS

(A Christmas Sermon)

"Now the birth of Jesus Christ was on this wise." Matt. 1:18

Of the Advent of Christ, Bengel wrote: "Oh, much-wished-for birth, without which we ourselves might well wish we had never been born!"

Christmas may be viewed from three angles:

1. As a date in history.

The very first Christians did not celebrate Christmas Day at all. When they started to do so, in the second century, they used a date in April or May. Others kept up the festival of the Epiphany—6th January. But somewhere about A.D. 330 the Christians in Rome decided to remember the birth of Jesus on 25th December, and that is the date we have kept since then.
—H. F. Mathews

2. As a fete in the year.
3. As a state of the soul.

128. THE MAGI

"Now when Jesus was born in Bethlehem of Judea in the days of Herod the king, behold, there came wise men from the east to Jerusalem, saying, Where is he that is born King of the Jews?"
Matt. 2:1

Speculation has been busy as to the identity of the wise men spoken of in the text.

Some hold that they were priests from Persia. There was certainly a priestly caste in that country known as the Magi.

Some allege that they were astrologers, prophets of a sort.

Some say that they were kings.

We do not know. Nor do we know their number. From the fact that they presented three sorts of gifts, we conclude that they were three persons, but the Bible does not tell us so.

Nor do we know their names. Legend calls them Melchior, Balthazar. and Caspar, but again we do not know.

Traditionally, they are supposed to have differed in three ways.

1. They differed in the races they represented.

Each stood for one of the

59

great groupings of mankind—
white, yellow, black.
2. They differed in the age
groups to which they be-
longed: youth, mid-life, old
age.
3. They differed in the gifts they
offered.
Gold, frankincense, myrrh.

129. THE UNEXPECTED HAPPENS

*"When they [the Magi] had heard
the king [Herod], they departed;
and lo, the star, which they saw in
the east, went before them, till it
came and stood over where the
young child was."* Matt. 2:9

Here we have the account of the
visit of the Magi to Jerusalem and
Bethlehem. Who were they?
a) kings?
b) astrologers?
How many were there of them?
Three? The three gifts suggests
that, but number is not stated.
The incident suggests the following
points:
1. Christ can be found by the
most unlikely people.
a) Not by Jews, but by pagans, as were the Magi.
b) Not from near at hand,
but from a distance.
c) Not by biblical students,
but by people with little
knowledge of God.
2. Christ may be found by the
most unlikely means.
A star!
3. Christ may be found in the
most unlikely place.
A stable!

—A. E. Phillips,
One Hundred Sermons in Brief
60

130. FIRE

*"He shall baptize you with the
Holy Ghost, and with fire."*
Matt. 3:11

Any authorized person can baptize in water. Christ reserves for
himself the prerogative of baptiz-
ing with fire.
Note four facts about fire:
1. It must be kindled from
above.
"Quite evidently," someone
may say, "you don't know
much about lighting fires.
They must be lit from below
the fuel if they are to burn
satisfactorily. Try lighting the
fuel at the top and you will
find that pretty soon the fire
will go out." That is a matter
of everyday experience. Yet it
may be true to say that all
fires are lit from above, because fire may have come
originally from the sun.
2. It must be maintained by mutual contact:

There is an old story of a clergyman
who was distressed by the growing
carelessness of one of his young men
in regard to church-going. He visited
him on a Saturday evening, and found
him comfortably in his room beside
his fire. In the course of conversation
the minister alluded to his anxiety, and
inquired into the reasons for the youth's
change in custom. The usual excuse
was offered: church-going did not help
him. To this the clergyman made no
audible reply. He simply took a pair
of tongs and lifted one of the coals
from the heart of the fire and set it
in the fender. No word was spoken.
The two men sat in silence and saw
the heat and colour fade away from the
coal, till it became a dead cinder. The

acted parable was enough. "I will be there again tomorrow," said the youth. The lesson had been learned.

—Lumsden Barkway

3. It wastes itself to give warmth to a cold world.
4. It transforms to its own nature everything it touches.

131. THE HEAVENLY RADIUM

"*The Holy Ghost and . . . fire.*" Matt. 3:11

Radium has been called "a bit of the sun imprisoned in the earth." Madame Curie discovered it.

In radium we may see a remarkable resemblance to the Holy Spirit.

The resemblance is fourfold:
1. There is a resemblance in that both are great producers of light.
   It has been estimated that a small fraction of an ounce of radium would illuminate a house for a century.
   The Holy Spirit is the Spirit of truth.
2. There is a resemblance in that both are great producers of power.
   Whereas it would take twelve thousand tons of coal to propel a liner for six thousand miles at a speed of fifteen knots, only twenty ounces of radium would be required to do it. The Holy Spirit is the Spirit of power.
3. There is a resemblance in that both are great agents of healing.
   Monsieur Becquerel tells that he had carried in his waistcoat pocket a small tube containing radium in order to show it to his friends. After a short time, he found the skin beneath his pocket red and inflamed. A painful sore ultimately developed. This at once suggested the use of radium to stamp out physical diseases. Cancers and ulcers yield to its application.
   The Holy Spirit is the divine healer.
4. There is a resemblance in that both are great self-communicants.
   The radioactivity of radium is well known, and the Holy Spirit yearns to communicate himself to men.

—Norman McLeod Caie, *The Secret of a Warm Heart*

132. THE COMFORT OF THE CHRIST

"*It is written.*" Matt. 4:4
"*It is finished.*" John 19:30
"*It is I.*"—Matt. 14:27

1. The comfort of his Word.
2. The comfort of his work.
3. The comfort of his abiding presence in the world.

133. CHRIST CALLING MEN TO THE MINISTRY

(An Ordination Sermon)

"*He [Jesus] saw two brethren, James the son of Zebedee, and John his brother, in a ship with Zebedee their father, mending their nets; and he called them. And they immediately left the ship and their father, and followed him.*"
Matt. 4:21-22

61

It is deeply significant that when Jesus was on earth he never delegated to others the task of calling men to be his ministers. He did not depute it to Peter. He did not refer it to John. He did not commit it to James. He kept it to himself.

He called them one by one as he summoned Matthew and Nathaniel; he called them two by two as he did Peter and Andrew, and James and John; he called the Twelve by name; he called the Seventy. Always it was *he* who called.

Of course, at the very beginning only he *could* call, and in the brief narrative which forms our text we see him summoning to his side two of his earliest followers.

Let us, with this story before us, observe four things about Christ's mode of calling men.

1. Christ calls busy men, not idlers.
   They were "mending their nets."
   When Jesus wants a minister, he does not look around for somebody with time on his hands: He summons the busiest man he can find!
2. He calls young men, not old.
   "They left their father."
   Billed to conduct a great evangelistic campaign, John McNeill got a telegram to say that his father had passed away in distant Scotland. The date of the funeral conflicted with that of the appointment. What would McNeill do? Would he cancel the engagement? Attend the funeral and leave someone else to carry on? No! Deeply devoted

though he was to his father, he felt that duty had the prior claim.

3. He calls cooperative men, not individualists.
   "Two brethren . . . in a ship."
4. He calls sacrificial men, not self-servers.
   "They . . . left the ship and their father."

134. GOOD FOR NOTHING

"Ye are the salt of the earth: but if the salt have lost his savor, wherewith shall it be salted? it is thenceforth good for nothing, but to be cast out, and to be trodden under foot of men." Matt. 5:13

1. The value of salt.
   "Salt is good."
2. The uses of salt.
   "Wherewith will ye season it?" There is no substitute for salt.
3. The perils of salt.
   "If the salt have lost its savor."

—J. Gregory Mantle, *God's Tomorrow*

135. PRAYER

"But thou, when thou prayest, enter into thy closet, and when thou hast shut thy door, pray to thy Father which is in secret; and thy Father which seeth in secret shall reward thee." Matt. 6:6

1. The period:
   "When thou prayest."
2. The place:
   "Enter into thy closet."
3. The privacy:
   "Shut thy door."

4. The Person:
"Pray to thy Father."
5. The promise:
"Thy Father . . . shall reward thee."

—Cornelius Woelfkin,
in *Snappy Sermon Starters*

136. THE DUTY OF FORGIVENESS

"If ye forgive men their trespasses, your heavenly Father will also forgive you." Matt. 6:14

Christianity clearly and emphatically enjoins the duty of forgiveness and we may be urged to its practice by many motives.

1. Because an unforgiving spirit is injurious to ourselves.
2. Because an unforgiving spirit is unjust to others.
3. Because an unforgiving spirit is offensive to God.
4. Because Christ specially requires us to forgive injuries done to us.
5. Because he makes our forgiveness of others the condition of being forgiven ourselves.

—Wilson T. Hogue,
A Handbook of Homiletics and Pastoral Theology

137. ANXIOUS CARE

"Take no thought."
Matt. 6:25 ff.

"Take no thought." This injunction rings out from the paragraph three times. By an examination of the context of each occurrence we learn that:

1. Nature shows that anxious care is needless.
Matt. 6:25-30
2. Revelation shows that anxious care is pagan.
Matt. 6:31, 32
3. Providence shows that anxious care is futile.
Matt. 6:33, 34

—Alexander Maclaren

138. THE WILD FLOWERS

"Consider the lilies."
Matt. 6:28

As we consider the lilies, we are constrained to utter four ejaculations:

1. How beautiful God's thoughts are!
2. How loving God's heart is!
3. How great God's power is!
4. How sure God's care is!

—David Burns, *God's Poem*

139. SUPREME PRIORITY

"Seek ye first the kingdom of God and his righteousness; and all these things shall be added unto you."
Matt. 6:33

What—if you will pardon the bluntness of the question—is first with you? What are you "out for"? What are you really seeking? Is it money? Is it pleasure? Is it fame? Is it power? Or what is it?
Our text tells us what it ought to be.
It presents us with three things:

1. A kingdom to be sought.
"Seek ye first the kingdom of God."
2. A law to be kept.
"His righteousness."
3. A promise to be proved.
"And all these things shall be added unto you."

63

140. JUDGE NOT!

"Judge not, that ye be not judged."
Matt. 7:1

A famous judge once stated that in ordinary life nothing astounded or disturbed him more than to observe the casual yet confident manner in which people sometimes pronounce a verdict on the character or conduct of others without weighing the evidence or even taking the trouble to find out what the facts are!

Our Lord, when on earth, must have felt something like that. As the God-appointed judge of all the earth, he was shocked to hear men glibly passing sentence on others, although utterly ignorant of the facts of each case.

So we find him saying: "Judge not!"

Note that:

1. We are not to judge anyone by an isolated incident in his life.
2. We are not to judge anyone by his circumstances.
3. We are not to judge anyone by other people's opinions of him.
4. We are not to judge people in the mass.
5. We are not to judge people by their achievements.

We are to leave all judgment to God.

141. IN, OUT, NO MORE OUT

1. Security.
   "Enter ye in." Matt. 7:13
2. Liberty.
   "He . . . shall go in and out."
   John 10:9

3. Stability.
   "Him that overcometh will I make a pillar in the temple of my God, and he shall go no more out." Rev. 3:12

142. THE DANGER OF A COURSE OF SIN

"Wide is the gate, and broad is the way, that leadeth to destruction, and many there be which go in thereat." Matt. 7:13

We see the peril of embarking upon such a course from:

1. The ease and attractiveness of its entrance.
   "Wide is the gate, and broad is the way."
2. Its agreeableness.
   Accommodated to everyone's inclinations.
3. Its popularity.
   "Many go in thereat," thus influencing one another.
4. Its certain issue in destruction.
   "That leadeth to destruction."

—Wilson T. Hogue,
A Handbook of Homiletics and Pastoral Theology

143. A MAN'S RELIGION IN TERMS OF BUILDING

"A wise man . . . built his house upon a rock. . . . A foolish man . . . built his house upon the sand."
Matt. 7:24, 26

Everyone likes to watch a building going up.

In early manhood our Lord served as a builder.

He tells a man how to make the most of his life.

1. The house on the rock shows the ideal.
   What the Lord wishes every man to do.
   a) the foundation, the basis —get right with God.
   b) the rising walls—get right with others.
   c) the storm, the time of testing—get right with self.
2. The house on the sand shows the actual.
   What a man does with his life, apart from God.
   a) no foundation, to ensure stability in a storm.
   b) no right relations to ensure usefulness.
   c) no inner strength to withstand a tempest.

—Andrew W. Blackwood,
Expository Preaching for Today

144. WHEN JESUS COMES

"When Jesus was come into Peter's house, he saw his wife's mother laid, and sick of a fever. And he touched her hand, and the fever left her: and she arose, and ministered unto them."
Matt. 8:14, 15

Here, if it were needed, is proof positive that Simon Peter was a good man! When his mother-in-law was ill, he brought Jesus to heal her!

How unlike that other man who, in like circumstances, sent an urgent, if ambiguous, message to his physician: "Dear Doctor, my mother-in-law is at death's door. Come at once and pull her through!"

When Jesus comes—notice what happens!
1. The feverish life finds calm. "The fever left her."
2. The feeble life finds strength. "She arose."
3. The idle life finds labor. "She . . . ministered."
4. The lonely life finds fellowship. "Unto them."

145. THE MASTER AND THE MULTITUDE

"When he saw the multitudes, he was moved with compassion."
Matt. 9:36

Some never see the multitude at all. Absorbed in their own cares and interests, they do not cast upon it so much as a cursory glance. Others look upon the multitude with indifference. Others, again, with contempt. Others, still, with a desire to exploit it.

The Master, when he saw the multitude, was moved with compassion.

Note some facts about multitudes:
1. Multitudes are magnetic.
   Someone has written: "The sight of a multitude is, in its way, as attractive as a magnet. We run to see the object which has gathered it together."
2. Multitudes are pathetic.
   Hitler said that human beings were sheepish—easily led, even to the slaughterhouse! Jesus said they were "as sheep not having a shepherd." Matt. 9:36
3. Multitudes are sympathetic.

65

A crowd is swiftly susceptible to emotion. People will weep | in a mass who would never weep in isolation.

MATTHEW 11–21

146. CHRIST'S GIFT OF RESTFULNESS

"I will give you rest. . . . ye shall find rest unto your souls."
Matt. 11:28-30

We find here:

1. Restfulness through worship. "Come unto me."
2. Restfulness through work. "Take my yoke upon you."
3. Restfulness through waiting. "Learn of me."

—Andrew W. Blackwood,
Doctrinal Preaching for Today

147. THE HEAVY LADEN

"Come unto me, all ye that labor and are heavy laden."
Matt. 11:28

How were these people heavy laden?

1. With the demands of the ceremonial law.
   To them Christ offers the rest of grace.
2. With the cares of daily life.
   To them Christ offers the rest of his realized love.
3. With the burden of sin.
   To them Christ offers the rest of pardon.

148. YOKES

"Take my yoke upon you, and learn of me."
Matt. 11:29

1. These words tell us of the constraints of Christ.
   "Take my yoke upon you, and learn of me."
2. These words speak to us of the fellowship of Christ.
   "Take my yoke upon you."
3. These words suggest to us the service of Christ.
   "We [are] workers together with him." II Cor. 6:1

—A. J. Gordon, *Grace and Glory*

149. THE PARABLE OF THE SOILS

"Behold, a sower went forth to sow."
Matt. 13:3

1. The beaten path shows the hearer who does not hear.
   The seed never enters the soil.
2. The rocky soil shows the hearer who does not think.
   The thin layer of soil over a substratum of rock.
3. The thorny soil shows the hearer who does not heed.
   The best of soil infested with thorns.
4. The good ground shows the hearer who really hears.
   The bountiful return from all the seed.

—Andrew W. Blackwood,
Expository Preaching for Today

150. THE MYSTERY OF GROWTH

"Another parable put he [Jesus] forth unto them, saying, The kingdom of heaven is like to a grain of mustard seed, which a man took, and sowed in his field: which indeed is the least of all seeds: but when it is grown, it is the greatest among herbs, and becometh a tree, so that the birds of the air come and lodge in the branches thereof." Matt. 13:31, 32

In this parable our Lord represents Christianity as:

1. Small in its beginning.
2. Slow in its progress.
3. Grand in its outcome.

—David Burns, *God's Poem*

151. THE PARABLE OF THE TREASURE

"The kingdom of heaven is like unto a treasure hid in a field; the which when a man hath found, he hideth and for joy thereof goeth and selleth all that he hath, and buyeth that field. Matt. 13:44

This parable may be interpreted from two points of view as follows:

1. The merchantman=Christ.
2. The field=the world.
3. The treasure=the church.
4. The purchase price=the Incarnation and Atonement.
   or
1. The merchantman=the sinner.
2. The field=the world.
3. The treasure=Christ.
4. The purchase price=all that the sinner has.

152. THE SOLITUDE OF JESUS

"He went . . . apart. . . . he was . . . alone." Matt. 14:23

Consider:

1. His solitude in prayer.
   "He was alone praying."
   Luke 9:18
2. His solitude in temptation.
   Matt. 4:1
3. His solitude in sorrow.
   His loneliness in Gethsemane.

   It takes two for a kiss,
   Only one for a sigh;
   Twain by twain we marry,
   One by one we die.

   Joy is a partnership,
   Grief weeps alone;
   Many guests had Cana,
   Gethsemane had one.

   —Fredric L. Knowles

4. His solitude in redemption.
   "He only could unlock the gate of heaven, and let us in."

—James Dinwoodie, *Illustrated Sermon Outlines*

153. BRIEF PRAYERS

"Beginning to sink, he [Peter] cried, saying, Lord, save me." Matt. 14:30

1. Sinking times are praying times.
2. Short prayers are long enough.
3. Our extremities are God's opportunities.

—Charles Haddon Spurgeon

154. THE SILENCES OF JESUS

"But he answered her not a word." Matt. 15:23

67

Observe that his silences were not due to:
- a) coldness or indifference.
- b) lack of something to say.
- c) preoccupation with his own concerns.
- d) a feeling of superiority.

But—

1. They were marks of his thoughtfulness.

   He never spoke idly or unadvisably, but weighed every word and was silent until the time came for speech.

2. They were trials of faith.

3. They were expressions of profound sympathy.

4. They were mute verdicts on the lives of those involved.

155. THE SILENCE OF THE WORD

"He answered her not a word."
Matt. 15:23

There is no wonder in the Gospels greater than the wonder of the silence of the Word. That he should ever have been dumb who is the eternal utterance of the divine is an inscrutable problem. No mystery is darker than the mystery of a mute Christ.

Silence is so completely contrary to his nature. Were noon suddenly to become midnight, were midsummer suddenly to become midwinter —the fact could hardly occasion more surprise.

Yet the Word was, and still is at times, silent. There are puzzling hours when, like the Syrophenician woman, we pray desperately to him, and when he "answers not a word."

In the epistle of Ignatius to the Ephesians there is a sentence which comes to mind in this connection. Here it is: "He that hath heard the word of Jesus truly, can hear also his silence."

The silences of Jesus are meaningful as well as his speech, and if we have heard his speech we can bear his silence.

Consider:

1. His silence in relation to his own early life.

   How much we should like to know about those silent years! Yet he did not lift the curtain.

2. His silence in relation to the future life.

   Since he had it in his power to tell us all about existence in the Beyond, is it not amazing that, knowing how eagerly we yearn for such a revelation, he said comparatively so little about it?

3. His silence in relation to the date of his Second Coming. This silence was, of course, due to the limitations into which he voluntarily entered at his incarnation, he did not know what the date was. As Man he did not know, but surely as God he did! Yet he did not disclose it.

But—those who have heard Christ's speech can bear his silence.

156. FOLLOW ME

Consider four recurrences of the phrase in the New Testament:

1. The "follow me" of consecration.

   "If any man will come after me, let him deny himself, and take up his cross, and follow me."   Matt. 16:24

2. The "follow me" of dedication.

"Go and sell that thou hast, and give to the poor, and thou shalt have treasure in heaven: and come and follow me."
Matt. 19:21

3. The "follow me" of identification.

"My sheep hear my voice, and I know them, and they follow me." —John 10:27

4. The "follow me" of separation.

"If any man serve me, let him follow me; and where I am, there shall also my servant be." John 12:26
—R. M. Pate,
in *Snappy Sermon Starters*

157. THE WORTH OF THE SOUL

"What is a man profited, if he shall gain the whole world, and lose his own soul?" Matt. 16:26

That solemn and searching question can become:

1. An epitaph.
   Describing the end of the man of ambition.
2. A danger signal.
   Which we ignore at our peril.
3. A staff to lean on.
   When the going is hard, and we are greatly tempted.

—E. D. Jarvis,
If Any Man Minister

158. CHRIST AND THE CHURCH

"Where two or three are gathered together in my name, there am I in the midst of them."
Matt. 18:20

1. The church of the Christ.
   a) its minimal number:
   "Two." John in the Book of Revelation was unable to give us the maximum, but Jesus has given us the minimum.
   b) its social element:
   "Gathered together."
   c) its inherent power:
   "In my name."
   d) its extensive area:
   "For where. . . ."
2. The Christ of the church
   a) His omnipresence:
   "There am I."
   b) His centrality:
   "In the midst."

—T. Morgan,
One Hundred Sermons in Brief

159. INSEPARABLE THINGS

"What . . . God hath joined together, let not man put asunder."
Matt. 19:6

1. God has united truth and love.
2. God has united privilege and responsibility.
3. God has united belief and conduct.
4. God has united submission and freedom.
5. God has united sin and punishment.
6. God has united faithfulness and reward.
7. God has united character and destiny.

—W. Graham Scroggie
in *My Way of Preaching*

160. WHAT GOD HATH JOINED

(A Marriage Sermon)

"They are no more twain, but one flesh. What therefore God hath joined together, let not man put asunder." Matt. 19:6

It is always fatal to part what God has joined. God has joined this planet to the sun: part them, and the earth rolls into ruin. God has joined the tree to the soil; part them, and the forest giant becomes a lifeless log. God has joined the human head to the body; part them, and you have a corpse. It is, I repeat, always fatal to part what God has joined.

Now in the Christian bond of wedlock a man and a woman are joined together not by a registrar or by a minister, but by God Almighty himself. Marriage is not, for the Christian, a mere legal contract, terminable at any time by mutual consent of the parties concerned, or by the infidelity of one of them. It is a spiritual experience in which two souls are made one by the Creator of them both. That is why the church has always taken such a strong line about divorce. Man must not put asunder what God has joined together.

Yes! God makes a man and a woman one in wedlock, but that does not absolve them from the duty of maintaining the matrimonial union.

How is this to be done?

1. See eye to eye.
   You say: "That begs the question." Maybe it does, but the couple that does not try to see eye to eye, never will!
2. Talk heart to heart.
3. Walk hand in hand.
   Don't merely tolerate one another's existence and go your respective ways.
4. Kneel side by side.
   "The family that prays together stays together."

161. THE TRIUMPHAL ENTRY

"And when they drew nigh unto Jerusalem. . . . all the city was moved, saying, Who is this?" Matt. 21:1, 10

We see here:

1. A sorrowing Christ and a rejoicing crowd.
2. A firm Christ and a fickle crowd.
3. A Christ advancing to the most glorious deed in all history; the crowd advancing to the most atrocious deed in all history. —Unknown

MATTHEW 22–28

162. WHY NO WEDDING GARMENT?

"Friend, how camest thou in hither not having a wedding garment?" Matt. 22:12

Perhaps:

1. Because it would not fit.
   The garment Christ gives fits all who apply for it.
2. Because it was too costly.

The garment Christ gives is bestowed free.

3. Because it was not fairly offered.

The garment Christ gives is graciously available to all.

—John Jones

163. THE CHRISTIAN'S GRAMMAR

"Thou shalt love the Lord thy God with all thy heart, and with all thy soul, and with all thy mind. . . . Thou shalt love thy neighbor as thyself." Matt. 22:37, 39

Bishop Taylor-Smith once gave a lesson in grammar to a congregation at Cambridge. "We have learnt to say, 'First person, I; second person, thou; third person, he,' " he said. "But that is wrong—so wrong indeed that to put it right one has to turn it the other way round. The Christian's grammar is: "First person, He; second person, thou; third person, I.""

1. First person—God.
2. Second person—one's neighbor.
3. Third person—one's self.

164. OUR OPINION OF CHRIST

"What think ye of Christ?"
Matt. 22:42

The question "What think ye of Christ?" can be asked from various angles. We can ask it, for example, in relation to the places associated with the main experiences and events of his life.
Thus:

1. In his cradle?
2. In his carpentry?
3. On his cross?
4. In his crypt?
5. Wearing his crown?

165. FOUR IMPORTANT THINGS

"These ought ye to have done."
Matt. 23:23

According to Henry van Dyke four things are essential to the full life of man. He puts the point poetically thus:

Four things a man must learn to do
If he would make his record true:
To think, without confusion, clearly;
To love his fellow-man sincerely;
To act from honest motives purely;
To trust in God and Heaven securely.

It is an excellent summation of human duty.

Let us look at it in detail together.

1. To think.
   "If there be any virtue, and if there be any praise, think on these things." Phil. 4:8
2. To love.
   "Thou shalt love thy neighbor as thyself." Matt. 19:19
3. To act.
   "Ye are my friends, if ye do!"
   John 15:14
4. To trust.
   "Have faith in God."
   Mark 11:22

166. THREEFOLD APOSTOLATE

"Behold, I send unto you prophets, and wise men, and scribes."
Matt. 23:34

71

The preacher is here presented to us as:

1. Speaker.
   "Prophets."
2. Thinker.
   "Wise men."
3. Writer.
   "Scribes."

167. FIVE WERE WISE AND FIVE WERE OTHERWISE

"And at midnight there was a cry made, Behold, the bridegroom cometh; go ye out to meet him."
Matt. 25:6

This parable instructs us as to:

1. The peril of externalism.
   "They that were foolish took their lamps, and took no oil with them." Matt. 25:3
2. The fact that Christian character is not transferable.
   "Give us of your oil." "Not so." Matt. 25:8, 9
3. The solemn truth that the present is the only time for preparation.
   "While they went to buy, the bridegroom came . . . and the door was shut."
   Matt. 25:10

—R. J. Smithson,
Night Tragedies of Scripture

168. WASTE

"To what purpose is this waste?"
Matt. 26:8

Sir Titus Salt was pacing the docks at Liverpool and saw great quantities of dirty, waste material lying in unregarded heaps. He looked at the unpromising substance, and in his mind's eye saw finished fabric of warm and welcome garments; and ere long the power of the imagination devised ministries for converting the outcast stuff into refined and finished robes.
—J. H. Jowett

Note that:

1. There is no waste in nature.
2. There is no waste in modern industry.
3. There is no waste in the Christian church.

In Lincoln Cathedral there is a window which is pointed out with pride. The story of it is this. The great artist of windows in the time in which the cathedral was built was putting some windows in it. As he made them he rejected many pieces of glass. A youth gathered up the rejected pieces, the broken pieces, and made the famous window.

—James Dinwoodie,
Illustrative Sermon Outlines

169. THE ADVOCATE

"Why trouble ye the woman? for she hath wrought a good work upon me." Matt. 26:10

In thus defending the conduct of the woman, Jesus was vindicating:

1. The beautiful as against the useful.
2. The original as against the conventional.
3. The particular as against the general.
4. The unconscious as against the conscious.

   "She did it for my burial."
   Matt. 26:12

   But she did not know it!

—James Stalker, *Sub Corona*

170. MARY'S MEMORIAL

"There shall also this, that this woman hath done, be told for a memorial of her." Matt. 26:13

In London there are many memorials to men. I do not recall seeing many to women. Three I distinctly remember—that to Boadicea on the Thames Embankment at Westminster, that to Queen Victoria opposite the front entrance to Buckingham Palace, and that to Edith Cavell at the south end of Charing Cross Road.

Here, however, is a far greater and more enduring memorial than any of these: "There shall also this, that this woman hath done, be told for a memorial of her."

In this narrative we notice:

1. Devotion to Christ displayed. "There came unto him a woman having an alabaster box of very precious ointment, and poured it on his head, as he sat at meat." Matt. 26:7
2. Devotion to Christ decried. "When his disciples saw it, they had indignation, saying, To what purpose is this waste?" Matt. 26:8
3. Devotion to Christ defended. "Why trouble ye the woman? for she hath wrought a good work upon me."
Matt. 26:10
—B. D. Johns,
Pulpit Notes (adapted)

171. THE SINGING CHRIST

"When they had sung a hymn, they went out into the mount of Olives." Matt. 26:30

Surely Jesus joined in! The "they" would seem to be all-inclusive in both clauses. "They" sang a hymn; "they" went out. In their sacred song the voice of the Savior blended. Beneath the shadow of the cross, he sang!

The famous artists of history have given us many marvelous portraits of Christ—all of them, of course, imaginary! I do not recollect that they have given us one of the singing Christ. I wish they had.

What, I wonder, was the pitch of the Master's voice? It might have been any one of the three available to men.

1. There might have been in his song the tenor note of joy at the accomplishment of his mission.
2. There might have been the baritone note of fellowship with his followers.
3. There might have been the deep bass note of passion.

172. BLOOD MONEY

"Then Judas, which had betrayed him, when he saw that he was condemned, repented himself, and brought again the thirty pieces of silver to the chief priests and elders, saying, I have sinned in that I have betrayed the innocent blood."
Matt. 27:3-4

Why was Christ betrayed for money? Not for the want of it, but for the love of it!

There are three things about this blood money that I want you to note:

1. It was money whose purchasing power was higher than

73

that of any other in human history.

With it was bought the Son of God.

2. It was money that nobody wanted.

a) Judas cast it down in the sanctuary. Matt. 27:5

b) "The chief priests . . . said, It is not lawful for to put them into the treasury." Matt. 27:6

3. It was money whose use was prophetic.

With it they bought a plot of land. The purchase of that bit of earth with the price of the blood of Christ was symbolic of the fact that by his death Christ has redeemed the world.

173. WHAT DOES CHRIST STAND FOR?

"Jesus stood before the governor."
Matt. 27:11

To that inquiry three broad replies may be returned:

1. He stands for the friendliness of the universe and the fatherhood of God.

2. He stands for the initiative of God in man's salvation and for the significance of human history.

3. He stands for the worth of human personality.

—Robert Ferguson,
Some Reminiscences and Studies

174. PILATE WASHING HIS HANDS

"Pilate . . . took water and washed his hands." Matt. 27:24

What was this histrionic act a sign of?

1. Abandonment?
Did it mean that he was giving up the struggle to save Jesus from the will of his enemies?

2. Appeasement?
Was it an effort to conciliate Christ's foes?

3. Announcement?
Was it the procurator's way of publicly intimating the innocence of Jesus?

175. SIMON OF CYRENE

"And as they came out, they found a man of Cyrene, Simon by name: him they compelled to bear his cross." Matt. 27:32

What is suggested by this incident in the story of the Passion?

1. It shows us the real humanity of our Lord.

2. It provides a type or parable of Christian life.

3. It indicates what delightful consequences can flow from the doing of a difficult or distasteful duty.

Among the early Christians Simon of Cyrene and his two sons, Alexander and Rufus, became well-known personalities.

—G. Howard James, *Neglected Incidents and Characters of the New Testament*

176. GOOD MORNINGS BEGIN WITH JESUS

"Jesus himself met them, and said, 'Good morning!'"
Matt. 28:9 ASV

74

Think of some of the good mornings that begin with Jesus:

1. The good morning beyond conversion.
2. The good morning of every day in the Christian's life.
3. The good morning of resurrection.

Say not "Goodnight," but in some brighter clime
Bid me "Good morning!"

4. The good morning of a new world.

177. THE SIN OF INACTIVITY

"All power is given unto me . . . Go ye therefore, and teach all nations . . . and lo, I am with you alway." Matt. 28:18-20

Here we have:

1. A directive which is plain. "Go ye."
2. A duty which is personal. "Make disciples."
3. A dynamic which is provided. "All power is given unto me."

—George B. Duncan,
Wanting the Impossible

MARK

178. THE DIFFICULTY OF FORGIVENESS

"Whether is it easier to say to the sick of the palsy, Thy sins be forgiven thee; or to say, Arise, and take up thy bed?" Mark 2:9

Some people seem to think that it is easy for God to forgive sins. Certainly Jesus did not. In this narrative in the New Testament we see him with a twofold problem on hand—around him a house crowded with critics and before him a helpless cripple, a man with a double malady, moral and physical.

Well, to heal the young man of his paralysis was no facile undertaking. It called for the exercise of supernatural power. Nevertheless, while fully aware of that, our Lord did not hesitate to put this question to the scribes then present: "Which is easier—to cure a paralytic or to forgive a sinner?"

The answer, of course, was that, to unaided man, both were alike impossible. No less than the healing of the bodily ailment, the cure of the sick soul called for the operation of divine omnipotence.

Why is forgiveness hard?

1. There is for God a legal difficulty.
   He must uphold the laws which he himself has promulgated.
2. There is a difficulty for the sinner himself.
   Memory and conscience make pardon seem impossible.
3. There is a difficulty in other people.
   God may forgive a man; the man may learn to forgive himself: but there are some people who will never forgive him.

75

179. WHY CHRIST CALLS DISCIPLES

"And he ordained twelve, that they should be with him." Mark 3:14

He calls them:
1. That they might hear what he says.
2. That they might see what he does.
3. That they might learn what he is.

—William Fraser McDowell,
In the School of Christ

180. HOW PEOPLE HEAR THE WORD

Mark 4:4-20

There are, broadly speaking, four types of listeners to preaching:
1. The lighthearted:
   The shallow hearer.
2. The fainthearted:
   The pusillanimous hearer.
3. The halfhearted:
   The double-minded hearer.
4. The wholehearted:
   The ideal hearer.

—John Eddison,
Christian Living

181. THE OTHER SIDE OF LIFE

"Jesus saith unto them, Let us pass over unto the other side."
Mark 4:35

1. Let us pass over from fear to faith.
   "Fear knocked at the door. Faith answered it. And, lo, there was no one there!"
2. Let us pass over from sin to salvation.
   "It may be that God can for-give sin, but I do not see how."   Socrates
   "By this man is preached unto you the forgiveness of sins."
   Acts 13:38
3. Let us pass over from time to eternity.

Katherine Tynan sings:

Some morning I shall rise from sleep
  When all the house is still and dark,
I shall steal down and find my ship
  By the dim quayside, and embark!

To no strange country shall I come,
  But to mine own delightful land,
With love to bid me welcome home,
  And love to lead me by the hand!

—W. J. Thompson,
in Church Management

182. TOUCHING CHRIST

"Who touched my clothes?"
Mark 5:30

This narrative reveals:
1. Christ's sensitive sympathy.
   A slight touch is enough to let him know that need appeals to him.
2. Christ's instant response.
   He meets the need without delay or question.
3. Christ's constant sacrifice.
   His miracles cost him virtue, the expenditure of vital energy.
4. Christ's gracious purpose.
   He not only seeks to heal the body, but also by such personal dealing as with the woman cured to assure of personal salvation.

—A. E. Garvie,
A Guide to Preachers

76

183. THE DRAMA OF A DYING SOUL

"Herod feared John, knowing that he was a just man and a holy, and observed him; and when he heard him, he did many things, and heard him gladly."   Mark 6:20
"It is John, whom I [Herod] beheaded: he is risen from the dead."
          Mark 6:16
"Herod with his men of war set him [Jesus] at nought, and mocked him, and arrayed him in a gorgeous robe, and sent him again to Pilate."
          Luke 23:11

There are three acts in this drama:
1. Act One: Conscience listening to the prophet.
2. Act Two: Conscience frightened of a ghost.
3. Act Three: Conscience callous before the challenge of Christ.

          —Unknown

184. CONTRARY WINDS

"He saw them toiling in rowing; for the wind was contrary unto them."   Mark 6:48

1. Sometimes winds are contrary because we are going in the wrong direction.
2. Winds contrary to us are favorable to others.
3. Contrary winds can call forth strength as we struggle with them.

          —Stanley H. Bailes,
in The Presbyterian Record

185. PROFIT AND LOSS

"What shall it profit a man, if he shall gain the whole world, and lose his own soul?"   Mark 8:36

Everyone engaged in business is familiar with the ideas of profit and loss. The businessman's whole concern is to secure the one and avoid the other. Before embarking on any enterprise, he does not only ask: "What will it cost?" He asks, to him, a still more important question: "What will be the profit?" And, provided the profit is assured, he feels perfectly safe in proceeding with the venture.

Yet, strangely enough, in connection with the biggest business of all—the business of living—so many people set about it without ever inquiring whether or not it is likely to be a profitable undertaking, or how to make it so.

In the text Jesus bids us stop and study that issue. "What shall it profit a man, if he shall gain the whole world; and lose his own soul?"

There are three things to be noted:
1. Gaining everything.
   "If he shall gain the whole world." Think of Alexander the Great, of Napoleon, of Hitler—they gained the world but lost their souls.
2. Losing the thing.
   "And lose his own soul."
   A story is told about a man who went to the diamond mines of South Africa, seeking diamonds. He found one so fabulously valuable that his fortune was made for life. On the way home to Britain, he traveled on a luxury liner. So elated was he by his success in discovering the marvelous diamond, that he got drunk and brought the precious stone on to the deck for the

77

other passengers to see it. Tipsily, he started playing with the diamond not far from the handrail surrounding the deck. A huge wave hit the vessel on its side. It lurched heavily, just as the man was tossing up his diamond. The diamond fell overboard and was lost in the sea!

Just so do some men trifle with their most priceless possession—their souls!

3. Profiting nothing. "What shall it profit a man?"

186. THE VALUE OF A SOUL

"What shall it profit a man, if he shall gain the whole world, and lose his own soul?" Mark 8:36

The value of the soul may be inferred from:

1. The marvelous construction of the body which is its casket.
2. The fact that Christ bought it at the cost of his own life.
3. The truth that its loss cannot be compensated for by the gain of the whole world.

—John Jones

187. SALT

"Salt is good." Mark 9:50
"Have salt in yourselves."
Mark 9:50

Salt is cheap and common, yet we cannot afford to despise it on that account.

1. Salt is good for counteracting what is bad.
2. Salt is good for its medicinal qualities.

About 120 grains are required daily by an adult to keep the system in order.

3. Salt, to do good, must be in its proper place.
4. Salt, to do good, must have lost none of its properties.

—John Mitchell,
Stones for Sermon Builders

188. SALT

"Salt is good." Mark 9:50
"With all thine offerings thou shalt offer salt." Lev. 2:13
"Seasoned with salt." Col. 4:6

It is somewhat surprising that the only article of diet which Christ pronounced good was salt. He did not say that bread was good; he did not say that water was good; he did not say that wine was good. But he did say that salt was good. Let us note one or two things about it.

1. Salt is something for which there is no substitute.
   "Salt is a thing on its own," wrote Lionel Fletcher, "a thing without a substitute. You do not compare salt to anything else, but other things must be compared to it. You may say, 'That is salty,' but if you say, 'That is salt,' you are immediately understood. So Christ desires it to be with His disciples."
   Salt is the thing you think of most when it isn't there.
2. Salt is something found all over the world.
   "Every ton of Atlantic water, when evaporated, yields 81 lbs of salt; a ton of Pacific

78

water, 79 lbs; Arctic and Antarctic waters yield 85 lbs to the ton; and the water of the Dead Sea, 187 lbs."

3. Salt is something which does its work in secret.
Its influence is subtle, yet pervasive.

4. Salt is something with several functions.
   a) It preserves.
   b) It flavors.
   c) It heals.
   d) It was used among the ancient Hebrews in the rites of the altar.

189. THE HERESY OF LIVING IN COMPARTMENTS

"What therefore God hath joined together, let not man put asunder."
Mark 10:9

We must not separate:

1. Sacred and secular.
2. Reason and revelation.
3. Comfort and challenge.

—Murdo Ewen Macdonald,
The Vitality of Faith

190. INHERITING

"Good Master, what shall I do that I may inherit eternal life?"
Mark 10:17

This young man had inherited so much. He had inherited wealth. He had inherited property. He had inherited rank. Very probably he had also inherited good health, education, and an ancestral religion. He had inherited so much that he had come to imagine that he could inherit everything. All he had to do was to present his claim and whatever he wanted fell like ripe fruit into his lap.

"Good Master, what shall I do that I may inherit?"

The Greek word in the original is an interesting one. It is *kleponomeso*, a word which suggests to the discerning two English words "kleptomania" and "antinomy." By putting together the ideas in the two parts of the Greek word we get the conception of acquiring by law.

Everything had come to the rich young ruler by law. His fortune had been conferred upon him in strict compliance with legal requirements. He had got everything by law—by inheritance. Could he not also inherit eternal life in that way?

But no. There was a higher law —the law of altruism—whose terms proved too exacting for him. The trouble with him was that he was essentially selfish. Even in his spiritual aspirations self was at the center. He was all wrapped up in himself. "A selfish man," wrote George Macdonald, "differs from an insane man in that while an insane man is *beside* himself, a selfish man is *inside* himself."

The rich young ruler was inside himself. Jesus challenged him to come out of that narrowing prison.

1. Think of the values to be weighed.
   Gold versus God.
2. Think of the price to be paid.
   "Go and sell all that thou hast."
3. Think of the choice to be made.
   "Come, take up the cross and follow me."

79

Many years ago when John A. Broadus, a master among those who know in the field of homiletics, was a student in the University of Virginia, he became friends with a fine young fellow who, though not a Christian, was of excellent moral character. One day the young man asked Broadus to write something in his autograph album. Broadus set down four words: "One thing thou lackest."

Do you lack that one thing?

191. THE CHALLENGE OF RELIGION

"Sell whatsoever thou hast, and give to the poor, and thou shalt have treasure in heaven: and come . . . follow me." Mark 10:21

Many have felt that Jesus was too hard on this youth. But this is more than Christ's challenge to one particular young man: it is Christ's challenge to the whole world.

1. It is the challenge of a person.
   Circumstances sometimes challenge us, but the most powerful challenges we encounter come to us from persons.
2. It is the challenge of a program.
   It was not just a matter of giving up, but of going on. The initial sacrifice demanded was but the vestibule to a life of sacrificial living.
3. It is the challenge to a passion.
   Nobody is going to make such a renunciation unless

gripped by a great enthusiasm. When we say that a man has a passion for music, for science, for money, we know what we mean. What is needed above everything is a passion for Christ.

—Sparks White Melton,
Will He Find Faith?

192. THE TRANSFIGURATION OF AMBITION

"And James and John, the sons of Zebedee, come unto him [Jesus], saying, Master, we would that thou shouldest do for us whatsoever we shall desire. And he said unto them, What would ye that I should do for you? They said unto him, Grant unto us that we may sit, one on thy right hand, and the other on thy left hand, in thy glory. But Jesus said unto them, Ye know not what ye ask. . . . Ye shall indeed drink of the cup that I drink of . . . But to sit on my right hand and on my left hand is not mine to give."
Mark 10:35-40

1. What James and John wanted.
2. The contrasting fact of what James and John got.
3. Yet what James and John got was what they wanted—but transfigured!

—Walter Russell Bowie,
Preaching

193. THE BLINDNESS OF BARTIMAEUS

"And they came to Jericho: and as he [Jesus] went out of Jericho with his disciples and a great number of

people, *blind Bartimaeus, the son of Timaeus, sat by the highway side.*
Mark 10:46

Consider the blindness of Bartimaeus as an analogy to the blindness of sin:

1. It was congenital.
   He had inherited it from his father. "Bar" means "son of." "Timaeus" means "blind." So with sin.
2. It was total.
   His blindness was not partial: he couldn't see at all. So with the sinner. "He cannot see the kingdom of God." John 3:3
3. It was social.
   That is, social in its consequences. The man was a beggar, a parasite on society, dependent on the charity of others for his very existence.
   Bartimaeus was not blind in a hermit's cave; he was blind by the side of a highway, blind in the midst of a crowd. So with the sinner. His evil doings have social consequences.

194. THE SPELL THAT JESUS CAST OVER MEN

"The common people heard him gladly." Mark 12:37

1. His was the spell of a man who knew.
   He always spoke with authority.
2. His was the spell of a man who was alive.
   Men constantly asked him about life.
3. His was the spell of a man who cared.

Everybody felt the love that beat in his heart.

—G. Campbell Morgan

195. ON DOING WHAT WE CAN

"And Jesus said, Let her alone. . . . She hath done what she could."
Mark 14:6, 8

From these words I wish to observe that:

1. It is everyone's duty to do what he can for Jesus Christ. This is so because:
   a) He is doing what he can for us.
   b) So many are doing what they can against him.
   c) After all, what we do will not amount to much.
2. Though you do what you can for Jesus Christ, someone is sure to find fault with you. But consider:
   a) With what kind of person the complaint generally originates.
   b) The form it usually takes.
   c) The spirit by which it is nearly always prompted.
3. Whoever finds fault, if you do what you can for Jesus Christ, you shall have his approval.
   Note that:
   a) He approves the motive and attributes the deed to love.
   b) He values the sacrifice and estimates it at its true worth.
   c) He immortalizes the ac-

81

tion and takes care to commemorate it.

—Thomas Davies,
Sermonic Studies

196. THREE SORTS OF PEOPLE

Mankind can be divided into three main groups—the thoroughly bad, those of whom it may be said that it would be good for them if they had never been born; the morally good, who are complacently self-righteous; and the Christians, who have been born from above.

There is a reference to each of these groups in one or other of the following texts:

1. Not born.
"Good were it for that man if he had never been born."
Mark 14:21
2. Once born.
"Born of the flesh."
John 3:6
3. Twice born.
"Ye must be born again."
John 3:7

197. THE NOSTALGIA OF JESUS

"And he [Jesus] . . . began to be sore amazed, and to be very heavy." Mark 14:33

There is a variant translation of a word in this text which seems to me very vivid and arresting. It is a translation for which there is, perhaps, slender warrant in the Greek, and yet a scholar of repute has seriously proposed it. Here it is: "He began to be sore amazed, and very homesick."

Homesick! Do you think Jesus was ever homesick? If ever he was, it must surely have been in dark Gethsemane.

"He began to be homesick." Why?

1. Because all through his earthly life he had never forgotten the glory of his eternal home.
2. Because the time had almost come for him to return thither.
3. Because in that shadowed garden he began also to be heartsick as he took on him the heavy burden of a whole world's guilt.

198. MEETING AT THE CROSS

"And they compel one Simon, a Cyrenian, who passed by, coming out of the country . . . to bear his cross." Mark 15:21

In many of our towns the common meeting point is the cross. "I'll meet you at the cross," one says to another, and at a prearranged time they keep the appointment at a place where the roads running through the town intersect. The cross is the venue.

It is the same, from the spiritual standpoint, with the cross of Christ. It is the great meeting place of history and destiny.

Observe how this is illustrated in the case of Simon the Cyrenian's encounter with it. Looking at that episode in the Gospels:

1. I see the divine and the human meeting at the cross.
2. I see the Savior and a sinner meeting at the cross.
3. I see the members of dif-

ferent races meeting at the cross.

4. I see successive generations meeting at the cross.

From the reference in Mark 15:21 it would appear that, as a consequence of Simon's conscription to carry the cross, not only did he himself become a follower of Jesus but also his two sons, Alexander and Rufus.

199. THE CONSCRIPT OF CALVARY

"And they compel one Simon a Cyrenian, who passed by, coming out of the country, the father of Alexander and Rufus, to bear his cross.   Mark 15:21

Simon, it has been said, is the patron saint of every Christian. We have all to carry a cross.

Notice four things about the cross-carrying of the Cyrenian which apply to our cross-carrying.

1. Conscripted.

Getting under that grisly gibbet was no part of Simon's personal plan as he journeyed to Jerusalem on that fateful morning. It was a disguised honor rudely thrust upon him. He was not a volunteer: he was a conscript.

2. Companied.

A point in the narrative not always noted is that, when carrying Christ's cross, Simon had Jesus for companion. In a spiritual sense Jesus was bearing for Simon what in a physical sense Simon was bearing for Jesus, and that made the bond between them at that hour very close.

3. Commissioned.

He who at first bore the cross because the rough Roman soldiery laid it inescapably upon his shoulders, afterwards took up the cross voluntarily and gladly which Jesus called him to bear. He was the father of Alexander and Rufus, two Christians evidently well known in the early Church. Simon was also the husband of one who acted the part of a mother to Paul. This makes it patent that Simon became an influential Christian.

4. Compensated.

Simon's only claim to immortality is his association with that Roman gallows. No doubt he shrunk from the horrible thing, as any sensitive person would. A hangman's rope would have the same effect on people today. But carrying that cross made Simon's name as imperishable as the cross itself. As long as the story of the death of Jesus is told, the story of Simon's cross-bearing will be told also. That, surely, is great compensation for an hour of public shame.

200. THREE ASPECTS OF THE RESURRECTION OF CHRIST

"He is risen."   Mark 16:6
"That I may know him, and the power of his resurrection."
                    Phil. 3:10
"Christ the firstfruits; afterward they that are Christ's at his coming."   I Cor. 15:23

Here we have presented to us three aspects of Christ's resurrection:

1. The historical.
2. The mystical.
3. The prophetical.

—A. E. Garvie,
A Guide to Preachers

201. THE GOD OF THE UNEXPECTED

"*These signs shall follow them that believe.*" Mark 16:17

There are three modern views of miracles:

1. Some say miracles are impossible.
2. Some say miracles are improbable.
3. Some say miracles are impolitic in the modern age.

But—Jesus says these signs shall follow!

—Charles Frederick Wishart,
The God of the Unexpected

LUKE 1–15

202. IF THERE WERE A SECOND BIBLE

"*Many have taken in hand to set forth in order a declaration of those things which are most surely believed among us.*" Luke 1:1

There is only one Bible. There will always only be one Bible. There is no need for another Bible. And yet sometimes, when I think of all that Christians have written since the canon was closed, I am almost tempted to wish that from among all that mass of literature materials could be found for a sort of second Bible.

Selecting items for inclusion in it would be a formidable task; but if I personally could have say in the matter, I should like to insert in its pages one or two uncanonical beatitudes.

The old Bible is, of course, full of beatitudes. Apart from the official ones, which form the prelude to the Sermon on the Mount,
84

beatitudes are scattered about the Book of God in generous profusion.

Three from modern writers that I should like to set in a new Bible are as follows:

1. Blessed are those who heal us of our self-despisings.
   —William Hale White
2. Blessed is the man who has found his work.
   —Thomas Carlyle
3. Blessed are the homesick, for they will come home.
   —Frank W. Boreham

203. HIS EXCELLENCY

"*It seemed good to me also . . . to write unto thee in order, most excellent Theophilus, that thou mightest know the certainty of those things wherein thou hast been instructed.*" Luke 1:3, 4

From this dedication of the Gospel of Luke we learn that:

1. The great of the earth need the gospel and need to be confirmed in its truth.
2. History has a way of reversing priorities.
   Who was Theophilus? Nobody knows. Who was Luke? The author of one of the four most important biographies in the world.
3. The memorable point in any man's life is his relationship to Christ.

—G. Howard James, *Neglected Incidents and Characters of the New Testament*

204. THE FIRST CHRISTMAS DAY

"And she [Mary] brought forth her firstborn son . . . and laid him in a manger, because there was no room for them in the inn." Luke 2:7

It was Christmastime. A minister and his wife had just had the misfortune to lose their eldest son, and as with other members of their little family they sat around the table at the festal dinner, they were sadly conscious of the empty place. Suddenly, one of their other children said: "This will be Howard's first Christmas in heaven, won't it?" Before either of the parents had a chance to reply, another of the little ones broke in: "Don't be silly. It's Christmas everyday in heaven!"

"Christmas everyday in heaven!" Yes, and for the true Christian it is Christmas everyday on earth. Still, after all, there was really only one Christmas Day, and that happened back in history, nearly two thousand years ago.

Note that:

1. On the first Christmas Day the greatest Person on earth was the smallest.
2. On the first Christmas Day the richest Person on the earth was the poorest.
3. On the first Christmas Day the most eloquent Person on the earth was speechless.
   Remember Tennyson's lines in "In Memoriam":

So runs my dream: but what am I?
   An infant crying in the night:
   An infant crying for the light:
And with no language but a cry.

At that first Christmastide the eternal Word was just an inarticulate Infant.

4. On the first Christmas Day the weakest Person on the earth was the strongest.

205. WHAT SHALL WE DO TO MARY?

(A Christmas Sermon)

"Yea, a sword shall pierce through thy own soul also." Luke 2:35

1. Shall we criticize her?
   That is what the scandalmongers did in ancient Nazareth.
2. Shall we canonize her?
   That is what the Roman Catholic Church does.
3. No! We shall recognize her for the good woman that she was, and thank God that she was willing to be the mother of the Messiah.

—A. C. Holt,
in *Snappy Sermon Starters*

206. THE LOST CHRIST

"Now his parents went to Jeru-salem every year at the feast of the passover. And when he was twelve years old, they went up to Jeru-salem after the custom of the feast. And when they had fulfilled the days, as they returned, the child Jesus tarried behind in Jerusalem; and Joseph and his mother knew not of it."   Luke 2:41-43

1. The last person lost him that we should have expected. His mother.
2. She lost him in the last place we should have expected. The church.
3. She lost him without at first being conscious of her loss.
4. She found him where she lost him.

—Quoted by Clovis G. Chappell in *Anointed to Preach*

207. CHRIST'S ANSWER TO HIS MOTHER

"How is it that ye sought me? wist ye not that I must be about my Father's business?"   Luke 2:49

We see here:

1. Life's highest relation. "My Father."
2. Life's highest occupation. "My Father's business."
3. Life's highest inspiration. "I must."

—N. Macleod, *One Hundred Sermons in Brief*

208. TO THOSE WHO ARE THIRTY-THREE

"Jesus himself began to be about thirty years of age." Luke 3:23

While looking through one of my old notebooks recently I came upon an entry made in it on the morning of my thirty-third birth-day. I had written: "It is a solemn thing to be thirty-three! At that age Jesus had finished his work. Have I even begun mine?"

1. Think of Alexander the Great dying at thirty-three, and see the futility of living for world-ly ambition.
2. Think of Lord Byron at thirty-three living for lust, and see the vanity of a life spent in sensuality.

   In his *Diary* under date January 21, 1821, he wrote:

Through life's road, so dim and dirty,
I have dragged to three-and-thirty;
What have these years left to me?
Nothing—except thirty-three!

3. Think of Jesus Christ dying at thirty-three, and see the glory of a life lived for God. "I have finished the work which thou gavest me to do." John 17:4 "It is finished." John 19:30

209. LAUNCHING OUT

"Launch out into the deep, and let down your nets for a draught."   Luke 5:4

We have here:

1. A strange command. The time for fishing was past, and the fishermen might have reasoned that surely Jesus did not know much about fishing or he would never give such an order.
2. A wonderful catch. Both ships were filled to over-

flowing with the fish, although some had escaped through the broken net.

3. A startling request.
"Depart from me; for I am a sinful man, O Lord."
Luke 5:8

4. A sudden call.
"Fear not; from henceforth thou shalt catch men alive."

5. A prompt response.
Peter, James, and John immediately forsook all and followed Jesus.

—John Mitchell, *Shot and Shell for the Preacher's Gun*

210. FOUR KINDS OF HEARERS

"*Take heed therefore how ye hear.*"
Luke 8:18

There are four different kinds of hearers of the Word:

1. Those like a sponge.
They soak up good and bad together, and let both run out immediately.

2. Those like an hourglass.
They let what enters in at one ear pass out at the other, hearing without thinking.

3. Those like a strainer.
They let go the good and retain the bad.

4. Those like a sieve.
They let go the chaff and retain the good grain.

—Thomas Boston

211. THE LOOSING OF LEGION

"*And they arrived at the country of the Gadarenes, which is over*
against Galilee. And when he went forth to land, there met him out of the city a certain man, which had devils long time, and ware no clothes, neither abode in any house, but in the tombs.*"
Luke 8:26, 27

The story of this poor demoniac has three chapters. We may entitle them respectively:

1. Shamed.
"Into what shame does sin bring us!"

2. Named.
"And Jesus asked him, saying, What is thy name? And he said, Legion." Luke 8:30
What a bad name sin gives us!

3. Tamed.
"They . . . found the man, out of whom the devils were departed, sitting at the feet of Jesus, clothed, and in his right mind." Luke 8:35
How wonderfully from every sin Christ delivers us.

212. CHRIST'S SPECIAL CONCERN

"*He that is least among you all, the same shall be great.*"
Luke 9:48
"*The last shall be first.*"
Matt. 20:16
"*This thy brother . . . was lost, and is found.*" Luke 15:32

Someone has discerningly said that Christ had a special concern for:

1. The least.
He said they should be greatest.

2. The last.
He said they should be first.

3. The lost.
   He said they should be found.

—Unknown

213. THE TRINITY OF LOVE

"Thou shalt love the Lord thy God with all thy heart, with all thy soul, and with all thy strength, and with all thy mind; and thy neighbor as thyself." Luke 10:27

Just as John 3:16 is the gospel in miniature, so Luke 10:27 is the law in miniature. You get the fragrance of a hundred roses in a drop of scent; you get the gospel in a few well-chosen words; and you get the whole duty of man in a few more.

1. Love of self.
   "Thou shalt . . . love thy neighbor as thyself."
2. Love of others.
   "Thou shalt . . . love thy neighbor."
3. Love of God.
   "Thou shalt love the Lord thy God."

—James Dinwoodie, *Illustrated Sermon Outlines*

214. THE PARABLE OF THREE TYPES OF PEOPLE

"A certain man . . . fell among thieves. . . . There came down a certain priest. . . . likewise a Levite. . . . But a certain Samaritan . . . came where he was.
Luke 10:30-33

Commonly we call this story of Jesus the parable of the Good Samaritan. But it is more. It is the

parable of Three Types of People. Glance at each in turn.

1. There are those who cannot look after themselves.
   The assaulted man.
2. There are those who can look after themselves.
   The priest and the Levite.
3. There are those who, at cost to themselves, take the trouble to look after others.
   The Good Samaritan.

215. THREE PHILOSOPHIES OF LIFE

"But a certain Samaritan, as he journeyed, came where he was: and when he saw him, he had compassion on him, and went to him, and bound up his wounds, pouring in oil and wine . . . and brought him to an inn, and took care of him." Luke 10:33, 34

Consider in turn the philosophies of the three types of person represented in this parable.

1. The robbers.
   Their motto: "What's yours is mine: I'll take it!"
2. The religionists.
   The priest and the Levite. Their motto: "What's mine is mine: I'll keep it!"
3. The rescuer.
   The Good Samaritan. His motto: "What's mine is yours: I'll share it!"

—A. Leonard Griffith, *What Is A Christian?*

216. AT HIS FEET

"Mary, which also sat at Jesus' feet, and heard his word."
Luke 10:39

88

1. The place of love is found at the feet of Jesus.
2. The problems of love are resolved at the feet of Jesus.
3. The perception of love is quickened at the feet of Jesus.

—George B. Duncan,
Wanting the Impossible

217. THE UPTURNED LOOK

"And it came to pass, that, as he [Jesus] was praying in a certain place, when he ceased, one of his disciples said unto him, Lord, teach us to pray."

Luke 11:1

1. Here were people who wanted desperately to pray. "The wing of the bird seeks flight, the fin of the fish demands water, the instinct of the heart is for God."
2. Here were people who wanted to be taught to pray. I remember one day meeting a friend who is a proficient organist. He had sat at the feet of the most distinguished organists in my little country. When I met him on this particular day he was unusually excited. He gripped my arm. "Whom do you think I heard last week? Marcel Dupre!" "Indeed!" I replied. "And what was he like?" His grip on my arm tightened. "When he had finished, I was convinced that I had never heard the organ played before!"
3. Here were people who wanted the best teacher they knew.
If Shakesperae were to teach literature, Beethoven music, Michelangelo art—that would be wonderful. But how much more wonderful to be taught by Jesus how to pray!

—J. Ithel Jones,
Temple and Town

218. THE LORD'S EXAMPLE IN PRAYER

"As he [Jesus] was praying in a certain place . . . one of his disciples said unto him, Lord, teach us to pray." Luke 11:1

Note here:

1. Our Lord bases prayer on God's fatherhood.
"Our Father." Luke 11:2
2. Our Lord looks on prayer as life's battlefield.
"Deliver us from evil."
Luke 11:4
3. Our Lord finds in prayer a new inspiration for service.
"For thine is the kingdom, and so forth."
Matt. 6:13

—George Adam Smith,
Forgiveness of Sins

219. THE PARABLE OF THE THREE FRIENDS

Luke 11:5-8
1. The friend who arrived.
"A friend of mine in his journey is come to me."
Luke 11:6
2. The friend who lacked.

89

"A friend of mine . . . I have nothing." Luke 11:6

3. The friend who supplied. "Friend, lend me three loaves." Luke 11:5

220. GOD'S GREATEST GIFT

"If ye then, being evil, know how to give good gifts unto your children; how more shall your heavenly Father give the Holy Spirit to them that ask him?"

Luke 11:13

1. The Holy Spirit is the greatest gift that God can give.
2. The Holy Spirit is the greatest gift that we can ask.
3. The Holy Spirit is a gift God won't refuse.

—W. E. Sangster,
in *Sermons I Should Like to Have Preached*

221. FRIENDSHIP WITH JESUS

"I say unto you my friends, Be not afraid." Luke 12:4
"I have called you friends; for all things that I have heard of my Father I have made known unto you."
John 15:15
"Ye are my friends, if ye do whatsoever I command you."
John 15:14

There have been numerous notable friendships in history. David and Jonathan, Damon and Pythias, Scott and Lockhart, Tennyson and Hallam—there are so many one could mention.

The greatest friendship in the world, however, is the friendship of the soul with Christ.

Notice what our texts tell us about that sublime companionship:

1. Friendship with Jesus banishes fear.
   That is the teaching of the first text.
2. Friendship with Jesus results in revelation.
   That is the message of the second text.
3. Friendship with Jesus carries a condition.
   That is the warning of the third text.

Wrote James Russell Lowell:

Moravian hymn and Roman chant
In one devotion blend,
To speak the soul's eternal want
Of Him, the inmost Friend.

222. THE DIVINE PROMETHEUS

"I am come to send fire on the earth." Luke 12:49

Prometheus is a titanic figure in Greek mythology who is fabled to have filched fire from heaven and brought it down to earth.

Christ, our heavenly Prometheus, did not steal the flame which he has sent among mankind. It is his own fire—the fire of passionate love.

Consider the following parallels between the gospel and fire:

1. The gospel, like fire, is in its essence profoundly deep and mysterious.
2. The gospel, like fire, brings with it many benefits.
3. The gospel, like fire, is intense in its working.
4. The gospel, like fire, is destined to ignite the world.

—H. O. Mackey, *Miniature
Sermons* (adapted)

223. ESSENTIALS

*"Except ye repent, ye shall all like-
wise perish."* Luke 13:3
*"Except your righteousness shall
exceed the righteousness of the
scribes and Pharisees, ye shall in
no case enter into the kingdom of
heaven."* Matt. 5:20
*"Except a man be born again, he
cannot see the kingdom of God."*
John 3:3

There are some things in the
Bible which do not seem very
clear, and therefore we have many
different interpretations of them.
The sincere truth-seeker does not
waste time on speculations, but
acts according to the clear and un-
mistakable commands of God.

1. Who are the perishing?
   "Except ye repent."
2. Who are the righteous?
   "Except your righteousness
   shall exceed."
3. Who are true Christians?
   "Except a man be born
   again."

—John Mitchell,
Stones for Sermon Builders

224. UNABLE TO ATTEND

*"They all with one consent began
to make excuse."* Luke 14:18

Fancy people excusing themselves from attending a banquet!
From a fast, quite likely, but not
from a feast! Yet that is the picture Jesus paints here, a picture
of people acting in a fashion in relation to spiritual things that they
would never dream of adopting toward natural things. And the
whole point is that they don't
know what they're missing!

Observe the nature of the excuses
proffered for nonattendance.
Three questions were raised:

1. The land question.
   "I have bought a piece of
   ground, and I must needs go
   and see it." Luke 14:18
2. The labor question.
   "I have bought five yoke of
   oxen, and I go to prove
   them." Luke 14:19
3. The love question.
   "I have married a wife, and
   therefore I cannot come."
   Luke 14:20
   Why didn't he bring her
   with him?

All these excuses are tendered still
by those who refuse to come to
the gospel feast. But who would
want an excuse for being absent
from a party?

225. PORTIONS

1. The sinner's portion.
   "Give me the portion of
   goods that falleth to me."
   Luke 15:12
2. The Christian's portion.
   The Lord is my portion, saith
   my soul." Lam. 3:24
3. The Lord's portion.
   "The Lord's portion is his
   people." Deut. 32:9

226. THE PARABLE OF THE THREE BROTHERS

*"This thy brother was dead, and is
alive again; and was lost, and is
found."* Luke 15:32

This matchless story that Jesus told commonly goes by the name of the parable of the Prodigal Son. Some have titled it otherwise. One, playing on the ambiguity of the word "prodigal," has labeled it the parable of the Prodigal Father. Others have referred to it as the parable of the Two Brothers. I do not recollect, however, that anyone has ever spoken of it as the Parable of the Three Brothers. Yet that is what it is, as I hope to show here.

1. There is the brother who strayed.
   The Prodigal.
2. There is the brother who stayed.
   The elder son.
   He stayed and was staid!
3. There is the Brother who paid.
   Jesus paid the price that all prodigals and elder brothers might come into the Father's house.

LUKE 18–24

227. A SERMON IN A PRAYER

"Men ought always to pray."
Luke 18:1

Hear this pertinent plea:
1. From the sensibility that shrinks from everything.
2. From the stolidity that is pleased with anything.
3. From the apathy that is touched with nothing.
   Good Lord, deliver us!

228. THE DUTY OF PRAYER

"Men ought always to pray, and not to faint." Luke 18:1

1. The text commands a duty which Carlyle called "the most stupendous act" of which man is capable.
   "To pray."
2. The text enforces the duty of prayer by an appeal to the supreme faculty of our nature.
   "Men ought . . . to pray."
3. The text suggests that, so far as we know, no other order of beings exists to which prayer is so imperative a duty as to man.
   "Men ought always to pray."
4. The text implies that success in prayer depends on that state of mind which ensures its constancy.
   "Men ought always to pray."
5. The text teaches that prayer is a resource in times of extreme emergency.
   "And not to faint."

—Austin Phelps, *Theory of Preaching*

229. IF JESUS WERE TO COME BACK TODAY

"When the Son of man cometh, shall he find faith on the earth?
Luke 18:8

92

If! But there is no "if" about it. Jesus *is* coming back. The supposition is not as to the fact but as to the fashion of his coming. If, however, he were to return, not as the New Testament says he will return, in power and great glory, but as he appeared at his first Advent, what sort of reception would he get from the people of our time?

Three men of the modern age have answered that hypothetical question in different ways.

Let us examine their replies to it each in turn.

1. The answer of Thomas Carlyle.

   He believed that men today would mock Christ's message. "If Jesus Christ were to come today," he said, "people wouldn't even crucify Him. They would ask Him to dinner, and hear what He had to say, and make fun of it."

2. The answer of Studdert-Kennedy.

   He believed that men today would treat Christ with indifference. He wrote:

When Jesus came to Birmingham,
They simply passed Him by,
They never hurt a hair of Him,
They only let Him die.

3. The answer of Arthur St. John Adcock.

   He believed that men today would try to evade the challenge of Christ by placing him on a pedestal. In his poem "The Divine Tragedy" Adcock paints an imaginary picture of the return of

Christ to earth, and describes particularly his adventures in London. He makes the citizens say:

It is far better He should only be
A tale we need not take too seriously,
An ideal throned above our fallen state,
For us to worship, not to imitate.

What is to be our answer?

230. A THREEFOLD CONTRAST

"*And he [Jesus] spake this parable unto certain which trusted in themselves that they were righteous, and despised others.*"
Luke 18:9

Here we have:

1. A contrast in the two men who went to pray.
   a) One was at the top of the ladder in church and state.
   b) The other was at the bottom.
2. A contrast in their prayers.
   a) One prayed "with himself."
   b) The other prayed to God.
3. A contrast in the results.
   a) One went as he came, hard and cold.
   b) The other went down remade.

—Clovis G. Chappell, *Anointed to Preach*

231. A STUDY IN CONTRASTS

"*Two men went up into the temple to pray; the one a Pharisee, the other a publican.*" Luke 18:10

93

Observe in this parable:
1. A contrast in personality.
   a) the ritualist.
   b) the secularist.
2. A contrast in posture.
   "The Pharisee stood and prayed thus with himself."
   Luke 18:11
   "The publican, standing afar off, would not lift up so much as his eyes unto heaven, but smote his breast."
   Luke 18:13
3. A contrast in prayer.
   "God, I thank thee, that I am not as the other men are." Luke 18:11
   "God be merciful to me a sinner." Luke 18:13
4. A contrast in preferment.
   "This man went down to his house justified rather than the other." Luke 18:14

232. THE BLIND MEN OF THE BIBLE

"And it came to pass, that as he [Jesus] was come nigh unto Jericho, a certain blind man sat by the wayside begging."
Luke 18:35

There are several blind men whose names appear in the Bible. There is Isaac, who in old age suffered from myopia and failed with his fumbling fingers to identify his son. There is Samson, "eyeless in Gaza," his career ending in tragedy because the Philistines have bound him and gouged out his visual organs. There is Saul of Tarsus, blinded by the glare and glory of the light he saw above the Damascus Road. There is, too, Elymas, the sorcerer, whom the apostle smote with blindness for a season because of his stubborn resistance to the word of God.

Of all the blind men in the Bible, however, there is none whose story moves us more than that of Bartimaeus.

1. Think of the deprivation involved in being blind.
   Not long ago the newspapers reported the case of a famous surgeon who has a daughter, born blind. The surgeon operated on the child and the operation was successful. Asked afterwards what was the most wonderful thing she had seen since receiving her sight, the child replied: "Daddy's face!"

2. Think of the danger involved in being blind.
   The wife of a Jew-hating and Jew-baiting Nazi leader was taken to a Christian hospital in Berlin during World War II to have a baby. Over the bed allotted to her was a picture of Christ. "Take away that painting," she commanded, "I don't want the first object my baby sees to be a picture of that horrible Jew!" "Sorry," the hospital authorities told her, "we are under orders and cannot remove the painting." In due course the baby was born. The picture was still there, and the mother, on returning to consciousness, looked at it balefully. "No need to worry about it," a doctor told her. "Your baby will never see the picture. He has been born blind!"

3. Think of the deception to which one is exposed through being born blind.

Many years ago, a blind man in business in a Welsh village was often handed half-pennies which he was told were sovereigns. It is despicable thus to take advantage of a blind man's disability, but who will deny that the thing is done, and every sightless man is exposed to it.

233. JESUS AT THE TREASURY

"And he [Jesus] looked up, and saw the rich men casting their gifts into the treasury. And he saw also a certain poor widow casting in thither two mites. And he said, Of a truth I say unto you, that this poor widow hath cast in more than they all. For all these have of their abundance cast in unto the offerings of God: but she of her penury hath cast in all the living that she had." Luke 21:1-4

Little though she realized it, that poor widow was watched by the incarnate God as she made her modest but munificent contribution to the temple fund that day.

Jesus was standing at the treasury. He always is.

1. He saw how little she gave. "He saw also a certain poor widow casting in thither two mites."

2. He saw that she might have given even less.
No one could have blamed her if she had given only one mite and kept the other.

3. He saw how much she gave.

He estimated the worth of the contribution not so much by what she gave as by the fact that, having given it, she had nothing left!

234. THE PUNCTUALITY OF CHRIST

"When the hour was come, he [Jesus] sat down, and the apostles with him." Luke 22:14

Consider that:

1. Christ was sometimes urged to act too soon.
a) Mary at Cana of Galilee: "Mine hour is not yet come." John 2:4
b) His brothers: "My time is not yet come: but your time is always ready." John 7:6

2. Christ was sometimes blamed for acting too late.
a) In the storm on Galilee: "Carest thou not that we perish?" Mark 4:38
b) At the death of Lazarus: "Lord, if Thou hadst been here, my brother had not died." John 11:21

3. Christ always acts at the proper time.

—B. D. Johns, *Pulpit Notes*

235. THE NATURE OF THE SACRAMENT

(A Communion Sermon)

"This do in remembrance of me." Luke 22:19

Three rhyming words convey to us, as well as any can, the nature of this holy ordinance.

95

Here they are: commemoration, communication, contemplation.

The Lord's Supper is:

1. Commemoration of an absent Lord.

   Christ's body is not on earth; it is in heaven. It is not dead on the altar; it is alive on the throne. So Peter says: "Jesus . . . whom the heaven must receive until the times of restitution of all things."

   Acts 3:20-21

2. Communication with a present Lord.

   "There am I in the midst of them." Matt. 18:20

3. Contemplation of a coming Lord.

   "Ye do show the Lord's death till he come."

   I Cor. 11:26

236. CHRIST TAKING BREAD

"He took bread." Luke 22:19

1. This bread pointed backward.

   Back to the manna in the wilderness.

2. This bread pointed upward.

   Up to the source of life from which it came.

3. This bread pointed forward.

   On to the Second Coming of the true Bread of God, Christ!

237. THE GENEROSITY OF JESUS

"He took bread . . . and gave unto them . . . Likewise also the cup." Luke 22:19, 20

Has it ever struck you that the only things Jesus is stated in the New Testament to have given to anyone were bread and wine? He did not give money, for the very sufficient reason that he did not possess any. He did not give clothing. (After his crucifixion, the soldiers gambled for his garments, but Jesus can hardly be properly said to have given the garments to them.) He did not give land or property. All he gave was bread and wine—bread when he fed the multitude and wine at the wedding in Cana. Both on the night of the institution of the Sacrament. Only bread and wine!

And yet, could any gift be greater? In giving bread and wine he gave the symbols of himself. No one can give more. "He took bread . . . and gave unto them . . . Likewise also the cup."

1. It was the consecration of the common.

   Every one of the disciples ate bread every day. It was the commonest article of food. Jesus consecrated the common.

2. It was the perpetuation of the passing.

   "This do in remembrance of me."

3. It was the spiritualization of the material.

   Not in the crude sense of the transmutation of the physical substance, but to the insight of faith.

   Only bread and only wine,
   Yet to faith the solemn sign
   Of the heavenly and divine.
   —Horatius Bonar

4. It was the universalization of the local.

The bread which Jesus then took and gave to His followers was simply an ordinary loaf, of very definite dimensions and occupying a limited amount of space. Yet, in some mysterious way, it was a prophecy that there would be "bread enough and to spare in the Father's house" till the last prodigal comes home. Not only then, in old Jerusalem, did Jesus give bread. He gives it at every sacrament the world over.

238. KNEELING FIGURES

"Every great movement of God," it has been grippingly said, "can be traced to a kneeling figure."

Consider three illustrations of this:

1. The kneeling Savior.
   "He [Jesus] was withdrawn from them about a stone's cast, and kneeled down, and prayed."   Luke 22:41
2. The kneeling pastor.
   "For this cause I [Paul] bow my knees unto the Father of our Lord Jesus Christ."
                        Eph. 3:14
3. The kneeling sinner.
   "Simon Peter . . . fell down at Jesus' knees, saying, Depart from me; for I am a sinful man, O Lord."
                        Luke 5:8

239. PENITENCE

"And the Lord turned, and looked upon Peter. . . . and Peter went out, and wept bitterly."
                    Luke 22:61, 62

What is penitence?

1. It is a divine thing.
   It began with God. Peter did not turn. But "the Lord turned, and looked upon Peter."
2. It is a very sensitive thing.
   A look did it. "The Lord . . . . . . looked upon Peter."
3. It is a very intense thing.
   "Peter went out and wept bitterly."
4. It is a very lonely thing.
   "Peter went out"—out into the quiet night, to be alone with his sin and God.
                    —Henry Drummond,
                        The Ideal Life

240. THE THREE CROSSES

"And when they were come to the place, which is called Calvary, there they crucified him, and the malefactors, one on the right hand, and the other on the left."
                        Luke 23:33

The three crosses of Calvary represent the crosses of humanity. On one of these three crosses every man is crucified.

1. The cross of selfishness.
2. The cross of self-surrender.
3. The cross of self-sacrifice.
                    —B. G. Newton,
                        Glimpses of God

241. THE THREE CROSSES

"And when they were come to the place, which is called Calvary, there they crucified him, and the malefactors, one on the right hand, and the other on the left."
                        Luke 23:33

1. The cross of a man losing his life.
   That of the unrepentant robber.
2. The cross of a man giving his life.
   That of the Redeemer.
3. The cross of a man gaining new life.
   That of the repentant robber.

—B. G. Newton,
Glimpses of God

242. THE THREE CROSSES

"*And when they were come to the place, which is called Calvary, there they crucified him, and the malefactors, one on the right hand, and the other on the left.*"
Luke 23:33

1. The sinner's cross.
2. The Savior's cross.
3. The saint's cross.

—B. G. Newton,
Glimpses of God

243. THE THREE CROSSES

"*And when they were come to the place, which is called Calvary, there they crucified him, and the malefactors, one on the right hand, and the other on the left.*"
Luke 23:33

1. The cross of punishment.
2. The cross of penitence.
3. The cross of pardon.

—J. W. Falconer,
The Three Crosses

244. THE UNIVERSALITY OF JESUS

"*And a superscription also was written over him [Jesus] in letters of Greek, and Latin, and Hebrew. This is the King of the Jews.*"
Luke 23:38

It was the common custom in those days, when a criminal was executed, publicly to placard his crime. As the man on the center cross on Calvary had been condemned for claiming kingly rights for himself, . . . the words of the charge stood written above his head: "This is the King."
But why the three languages?

1. It was written in Greek, the language of culture.
   Is Jesus king there?
2. It was written in Latin, the language of government.
   Is Jesus king there?
3. It was written in Hebrew, the language of religion.
   Is Jesus king there?

—James S. Stewart,
in *Modern Sermons*

245. THE WESTWARD ROAD

(A Wedding Sermon)

"*And, behold, two of them went that same day to a village called Emmaus, which was from Jerusalem about three-score furlongs.*"
Luke 24:13

This is one of the loveliest stories in the world. It is more. It is a parable of life. In it, we see two wayfarers trudging along the westward road, the road that leads to the sunset and the evening star.

Who were they? The name of the one we know. It was Cleopas. The other is anonymous. And because we do not know the name of the second traveler, there has been a good deal of speculation as to his possible identity.

Some say it was Peter, some that it was Nathanael, some that it was Luke himself. But there is a fourth view—that of those who suggest that it was probably the wife of Cleopas—and this I personally find by far the most attractive and convincing supposition.

That picture of the two travelers —a husband and his wife—making their way together along the westering road, appeals strongly to the imagination and lays a strange spell upon the heart.

Let us look for a little at that westering road.

1. It is a road on which we all must travel.
   None of us is traveling east; all are faring west.
2. It is a road on which, for one reason or another, we all tend at times to be sad.
   "What manner of communications are these that ye have one to another, as ye walk, and are sad?" Luke 24:17

3. It is a road, nevertheless, on which all of us may meet a mysterious stranger, who knows the answers to all our problems and who offers us his friendship.
   "Art thou only a stranger in Jerusalem, and hast not known the things which are come to pass there in these days?" Luke 24:18
4. It is a road that leads home at last.
   "And they drew nigh unto the village, whither they went." Luke 24:28

246. THE SUPREME EXPOSITOR

"Beginning at Moses and all the prophets, he expounded unto them in all the Scriptures the things concerning himself." Luke 24:27

1. Christ was the preacher.
2. Christ was the text.
3. Christ was the sermon.

Result: "Did not our heart burn within us?" Luke 24:32

JOHN 1–9

247. WHEN CHRIST CAME

"He came unto his own."
John 1:11

What more natural! "He came unto his own." Where else would we expect him to come? It was his own before he came, but he made it his own in a new sense by his coming.

Think of the difference that coming made to the world:

1. It was light coming into a world of darkness.
2. It was love coming into a world of hate.
3. It was life coming into a world of death.

248. WHAT IS THE CHRISTIAN LIFE?

"Behold the Lamb of God."
John 1:29
"Lay hold on eternal life."
I Tim. 6:12
"Holding forth the word of life."
Phil. 2:16

It is always difficult to sum up the Christian experience in a few words. These three texts, with their key words, seem to me to come as close to doing it as possible.

Of the Christian life they say that:
1. It is a vision.
   "Behold."
2. It is a venture.
   "Lay hold."
3. It is a vocation.
   "Hold forth."

—A. Lindsay Glegg,
Walking on Two Feet

249. THE INCARNATION OF THE HOLY SPIRIT

"I saw the Spirit." John 1:32

Our Lord made himself manifest to human eyes by assuming the form of man; the Holy Spirit, by assuming the form of a dove.

What is there about a dove which makes it an apt incarnation of the Spirit?
1. Its beauty.
2. Its vitality.
   We think of it as brooding, bringing life to birth.
3. Its tranquility.
   The dove is the symbol of peace.
4. Its affinity.
   It mourns pathetically for its absent mate.

100

5. Its sagacity.
   This is seen in its highly developed homing instinct.

—John Mitchell, *Shot and Shell for the Preacher's Gun* (adapted)

250. THE MAN OF THE SECRET LIFE

"Because I said unto thee, I saw thee under the fig tree, believest thou? Thou shalt see greater things than these." John 1:50

Here we have:
1. An insight into Nathanael's present.
   "Behold an Israelite indeed, in whom is no guile!"
   John 1:47
2. A supernatural knowledge of his past.
   "When thou wast under the fig tree, I saw thee."
   John 1:48
3. A glorious prophecy of his future.
   "Hereafter ye shall see heaven open, and the angels of God ascending and descending upon the Son of Man."
   John 1:51

—W. Mackintosh Mackay,
The Men Whom Jesus Made

251. CHRIST'S KNOWLEDGE OF MAN

"[He] needed not that any should testify of man; for he knew what was in man." John 2:25

1. He knew all the evil that was in man.
2. He knew all the goodness that was in man.

3. He knew all the moral possibilities that there were in man through grace.

—Z. Mather,
The Christ of the Heart

252. THE "CANNOTS" OF THE NEW TESTAMENT

"He cannot see the kingdom."
John 3:3
"He cannot understand the things of God." I Cor. 2:14
"He cannot be my disciple."
Luke 14:27

On the lips of an omnipotent God the word "cannot" is a mighty meaningful term!

Note the following occurrences of it in the New Testament:

1. The cannot of regeneration. "He cannot see the kingdom."
   In one of his sermons, F. W. Robertson has penetratively pointed out that these words denote not prohibition but impossibility. Jesus does not say, "He shall not," but, "He cannot."
2. The cannot of realization. "He cannot understand the things of God."
   A mother can interpret her child's letter far better than the most skillful and erudite grammarian. So spiritual things are spiritually discerned.
3. The cannot of renunciation. "He cannot be my disciple." When Jesus invites us to join him, as Dietrich Bonhoeffer has strikingly reminded us, "He bids us come and die."

253. A NEW BEGINNING

"No one can see God's Realm unless he is born from above."
John 3:3b Moffatt

"The only way to get into God's family," D. L. Moody used to say, "is to be born into it."

Think of:

1. The need for a new beginning.
2. The new beginning from above.
3. The birth from above as a mystery.
4. The mystery as a fact of experience.

—Andrew W. Blackwood,
Doctrinal Preaching for Today

254. BLESSINGS OF THE NEW BIRTH

"Ye must be born again."
John 3:7
"Therefore if any man be in Christ, he is a new creature."
II Cor. 5:17
"Behold, I make all things new."
Rev. 21:5

What are the special blessings of the New Birth?

Let me name four:

1. The blessing of a new home.
2. The blessing of a new heart.
3. The blessing of a new help.
4. The blessing of a new hope.

—William Fitch,
Enter Into Life

255. BRIEF BIBLE

"For God so loved the world, that he gave his only begotten Son, that

whosoever believeth in him should not perish, but have everlasting life." John 3:16

Here we have:

1. The fact.
   "God so loved the world."
2. The act.
   "That he gave his only begotten Son."
3. The pact.
   "That whosoever believeth on him should not perish, but have everlasting life."

—Unknown

256. THE FOUR GIFTS

There are four distinct gifts mentioned in the New Testament.

1. The gift of Christ by God to the world.
   "For God so loved the world, that he gave his only begotten Son." John 3:16
2. The gift of the church by the Father to Christ.
   "The men which thou gavest me out of the world." John 17:6
3. The gift of the believer of himself to God.
   "First [they] gave their own selves to the Lord." II Cor. 8:5
4. The gift of the Holy Spirit by Christ to the believer.
   "Ye shall receive the gift of the Holy Ghost." Acts 2:38

—A. Lindsay Glegg,
Walking on Two Feet

257. THE GOSPEL OF LOVE

"For God so loved the world, that he gave his only begotten Son, that

whosoever believeth in him should not perish, but have everlasting life." John 3:16

Many years ago a London preacher took as text this miniature Bible of a verse, and of it he made three points:

1. God's love is for the unlovely. Few think themselves such, but such we all are.
2. God's love is for the undeserving. It is for those who have no claim whatever to be loved.
3. God's love is for the undesiring. It is for those who do not even want to be loved.

—Unknown

258. THE COMING OF THE LIGHT

"This is the condemnation, that light is come into the world, and men loved darkness rather than light, because their deeds were evil." John 3:19

We see here:

1. Light conferred.
   "Light is come into the world."
2. Darkness preferred.
   "Men loved darkness rather than light."
3. Guilt inferred.
   "Because their deeds were evil."

259. A MUST IN THE LIFE OF THE MASTER

"He must needs go through Samaria." John 4:4

102

Why? He must needs go:
1. To dispense a blessing.
2. To correct a prejudice.
3. To proclaim a truth.
4. To set an example.

—Unknown

260. MUSTS IN THE MASTER'S LIFE

1. The must of service.
"He must needs go through Samaria." John 4:4
2. The must of sacrifice.
"So must the Son of man be lifted up." John 3:14
3. The must of sovereignty.
"He must reign." I Cor. 15:25

261. THE LIVING WATER

It is:
1. For us as a gift.
"If thou knewest the gift of God, and who it is that saith to thee, Give me to drink; thou wouldest have asked of him, and he would have given thee living water." John 4:10
2. In us as a well.
"The water that I shall give him shall be in him a well of water springing up into everlasting life." John 4:14
3. From us as rivers.
"He that believeth on me, as the Scripture hath said, out of his belly shall flow rivers of living water." John 7:38

—George W. Noble,
750 Sermon Outlines

262. THE WORTH OF WORSHIP

"*The hour cometh, and now is, when the true worshippers shall worship the Father in spirit and in truth.*" John 4:23

What is the worth of worship?
1. Worship frees us from the prison of self-centeredness.
2. Worship imparts to us a true sense of values.
3. Worship promotes in us a feeling of gratitude.
4. Worship relates our little lives to eternity.

263. AT THE SPA

"*While I am coming, another steppeth down before me.*" John 5:7

At a famous spa near Jerusalem a great multitude of sufferers had gathered together waiting to benefit from the waters.

One man, an invalid for thirty-eight years, was having a most frustrating experience. Whenever he tried to get into the pool, he was forestalled. Others, as we say, "beat him to it."

Many are like that in the vital matter of decision for Christ. They are always going to surrender to his claims, but they never do.

Why? The reasons may be similar to those which prevented the man in this narrative from entering the healing pool.

1. It may be sheer procrastination.
"He had been now a long time in that case."
John 5:6

2. It may be looking to man.
"Sir, I have no man."
John 5:7

3. It may be love for one's infirmity.
This is implied in Christ's question: "Wilt thou be made whole?" But note: though the man could not find healing, healing found the man in Christ.

—John Mitchell, *Shot and Shell for the Preacher's Gun* (adapted)

264. THE GOSPEL ACCORDING TO CHRIST'S ENEMIES

"*The Jews sought . . . to kill him, because he . . . said . . . that God was his Father, making himself equal with God.*" John 5:18
"*Is not this the carpenter, the son of Mary, the brother of James, and Joses, and of Juda, and Simon?*" Mark 6:3
"*He saved others; himself he cannot save.*" Mark 15:31

It is one of the ironies of Christian history that Christ's bitterest critics and opponents became unwillingly and even unwittingly among his most effective witnesses. There is a gospel according to Christ's enemies. Whatever suspicion might arise in the minds of modern skeptics to the testimony of his friends, none surely can affect that of his foes.

What, then, is the gospel according to Christ's enemies?

1. It is a gospel of Christ's Deity.
"Making himself equal with God."

2. It is a gospel of Christ's humanity.
"Is not this the carpenter?"

3. It is a gospel of Christ's Saviorhood.
"He saved others."

265. NOTHING— EVERYTHING

"*I can of mine own self do nothing.*" John 5:30
"*Without me ye can do nothing.*" John 15:5
"*I can do all things through Christ.*" Phil. 4:13

1. Apart from the Father, Christ himself could not achieve good.
2. Without Christ, his disciples cannot achieve any good.
3. The power that Christ had from the Father he communicates to his disciples.

—R. J. Wardell, *A Manual of Sermon Construction*

266. A LAD HERE

"*There is a lad here, which hath five barley loaves, and two small fishes: but what are they among so many?*" John 6:9

Here we have:

1. A lad.
2. A lad with a little.
3. A lad listening.
4. A lad letting go.
Note his compensation: For whom were the twelve baskets of fragments which the disciples gathered up after the crowd had been fed? We are not expressly told. But I suspect they were for the little

lad who had surrendered his lunch. "God is no man's debtor."

—Robert G. Lee,
Whirlwinds of God

267. WHAT IS YOUR VIEW OF RELIGION?

"*I am the bread of life.*"
John 6:35

1. Religion as fantasy.
2. Religion as luxury.
3. Religion as necessity.

—Murdo Ewen Macdonald,
The Vitality of Faith

268. THE BREAD OF LIFE

"*I am the bread of life.*"
John 6:48

We live in a hungry world. In nature everything has its mouth open—from the fluffy fledgling in the nest to the mighty monarch of the skies; from the minute minnow in the creek to the gigantic whale in midocean; from the nibbling mouse in the barn to the colossal elephant in the jungle—everything in nature is hungry, famished, ravenous.

Man shares with the lower orders of creation this elemental physical need. He too is conscious of natural hunger. But he is aware of something more, a higher hunger, the hunger of the soul; and this hunger none but Christ can satisfy. He says: "I am the bread of life."

This comparison by Christ of himself to bread I find very suggestive. In it I see:

1. The combination of heaven and earth.
   It takes heaven and earth to make bread.
2. The combination of unity and multiplicity.
   Christ is one, yet he has many members.
3. The combination of death and life.
4. The combination of wholeness and brokenness.

269. THROUGH DEED TO CREED

"*If any man will do his will, he shall know of the doctrine.*"
John 7:17

Someone has said that the coat of arms of the twentieth century is an interrogation point rampant above three bishops dormant, and its motto is "Query."

There are, of course, two types of doubters.

1. Willing doubters.
   To this class belong those whose wish is father to the doubt.
   To this class also belong those whose doubt is based on ignorance.
   You do not measure the fragrance of a rose by a yardstick, nor tell the power of a sunbeam by its weight upon the scales. If a man will take down the shutters of his soul, the darkness of doubt will go out before the light.
2. Unwilling doubters.
   Consider three New Testament examples of this class of doubter:

105

a) Nicodemus.
b) Thomas.
c) Cleopas and his companion on the way to Emmaus.

—Charles L. Goodell,
Pathways to the Best

270. THE DIVINE WATER CARRIER

"In the last day, that great day of the feast, Jesus stood and cried, saying, If any man thirst, let him come unto me, and drink. He that believeth on me, as the Scripture hath said, out of his belly shall flow rivers of living water."

John 7:37, 38

Often in the hot streets of Jerusalem the cry of the water carrier could be heard. "If you are thirsty, come to me and I will give you to drink." One day a divine water carrier appeared in that subtropical city offering water of a different kind.

In our text we have:

1. Thirst.
   "If any man thirst."
2. Supply.
   "Let him come unto me, and drink."
3. Overflow.
   "Out of his belly shall flow rivers of living water."

—C. O. Eldridge,
The Lay Preacher's Handbook
(adapted)

271. SPIRITUAL THIRST

"If any man thirst, let him come unto me, and drink."

John 7:37

It is a terrible thing to thirst. Equally, in certain circumstances, it is a terrible thing not to thirst. Do we thirst for the water of everlasting life?

1. Before the thirst, the supply.
   "If any man thirst, let him come unto me." John 7:37
2. For the thirst, the sufficiency.
   "The water that I shall give him shall be in him a well of water springing up into everlasting life." John 4:14
3. From the thirst, the surplus.
   "Out of his belly shall flow rivers of living water."

John 7:38

272. JESUS AS A PUBLIC SPEAKER

"The officers answered, Never man spake like this man." John 7:46

1. The world had never before heard a man like this speak.
2. The world had never before heard a man with things to speak like this man.
3. This man will speak when every other man has been silenced.

—W. Price,
Sketches of Sermons

273. CLEARER VISIONS THROUGH CHRIST

"One thing I know, that, whereas I was blind, now I see."

John 9:25

Christ makes clearer for us:

1. The vision of society.
2. The vision of self.
3. The vision of the Savior.

—John D. Hughes,
One Hundred Sermons in Brief

274. THE INTEGRATED LIFE

"One thing I know." John 9:25

Of the formerly blind man in this narrative it can be said that:

1. He had an assurance. *"I know."*

2. He had a personal assurance. *"I know."*

3. He had a simple personal assurance. *"One thing I know."*

—A. Skevington Wood, *Heralds of the Gospel*

JOHN 10–15

275. FOUR CLASSES OF PEOPLE

"A stranger will they not follow." John 10:5
"All that ever came before me are thieves and robbers." John 10:8
"The hireling fleeth, because he is a hireling." John 10:13
"I am the good shepherd." John 10:11

1. Strangers.
   Those who are indifferent to others.
2. Robbers.
   Those who prey on others.
3. Hirelings.
   Those who serve others for what they can get out of them.
4. Shepherds.
   Those who give themselves freely for others.

276. IN AND OUT

"I am the door: by me if any man enter in, he shall be saved, and shall go in and out, and find pasture." John 10:9

The ideal child of God is one who habituates himself to the regular and proper use of the Christ-door, to going in and out.

1. *In* to the shelter of the Christian faith and *out* to the exposure of it.
2. *In* to the restraints of religion and *out* to the liberties of it.
3. *In* to close-up views of the sheepfold and *out* to long vistas of the pasture.

Christ for the world we sing,
The world to Christ we bring.
—Samuel Wolcott

—Ralph W. Sockman,
The Unemployed Carpenter

277. CHRIST, THE HOMELESS ONE, OFFERING A HOME TO US ALL

"I am the door: by me if any man enter in, he shall be saved, and shall go in and out, and find pasture." John 10:9

It was distressing to learn that at Christmas 1962 there were a thousand homeless children in London. Housing should be given priority in every political program. When people tell me that a nation is great, I do not ask to see the most splendid architecture of which it can boast; I ask to see the home of its poorest inhabitant.

Christ offers a spiritual home to us all. There need be no homelessness of the soul.

Note three things about the home which Christ provides:

1. I find security in this home. "He shall be saved."
2. I find liberty in this home. "[He] shall go in and out."
3. I find plenty in this home. "And find pasture."

278. CHRIST—THE DOOR

"I am the door: by me if any man enter in, he shall be saved, and shall go in and out, and find pasture." John 10:9

Perhaps it was because he was a carpenter, I don't know, but it is certainly a fact that Jesus had much to say about doors.

Sometimes he pictured himself inside the door. This was the scene which he visualized when he said: "Knock, and it shall be opened unto you" (Luke 11:9), and when he told the story of the ten bridesmaids, which ends with the sad note: "The door was shut" (Matt. 25:10).

Sometimes he pictured himself on the outside of the door. That is his position in Rev. 3:20: "Behold, I stand at the door and knock: if any man hear my voice, and open the door, I will come in to him, and will sup with him, and he with me."

Here he pictures himself neither inside nor outside the door, but as the door itself. "I am the door."

108

Notice three things about a door:

1. A door divides.

It separates very sharply and finally separates those inside from those outside. Jesus does that. He divides men as well as uniting them.

"He is called a door," says Cyril, "but take not the name literally for a thing of wood, but a spiritual, living Door, discriminating those who enter in."

2. A door admits.

"By me if any man enter in."

3. A door excludes.

Jesus is not just a breach in the wall through which we may pass, one way or the other, just as and when we choose. He is the door. It is now open, but it may be shut.

Late, late, so late!
and dark the night and chill!
Late, late, so late!
but we can enter still.
Too late, too late!
ye cannot enter now.

No light had we;
for that we do repent,
And, learning this,
this bridegroom will relent.
Too late, too late!
ye cannot enter now.

No light! So late!
and dark and chill the night!
O, let us in, that we may
find the light!
Too late, too late!
ye cannot enter now.

Have we not heard
the bridegroom is so sweet?
O, let us in, tho' late,
to kiss his feet!

No, no, too late!
ye cannot enter now.

—Alfred, Lord Tennyson

D. T. Niles bids us note that Jesus does not say, "I am the fire-escape, the emergency exit," but, "I am the door."

279. THE LORD'S DEATH

(As predicted by himself.)
For whom did he die?

1. For the sheep.
   "I am the good shepherd: the good shepherd giveth his life for the sheep." John 10:11
2. For many.
   "The Son of man came not to be ministered unto, but to minister, and to give his life a ransom for many."
   Matt. 20:28
3. For the world.
   "I am the living bread which came down from heaven: if any man eat of this bread, he shall live for ever: and the bread that I will give is my flesh . . . for the life of the world." John 6:51

280. WHEN CHRIST IS ABSENT

"I was not there." John 11:15

Our theme is the absent Christ. Note that:

1. Problems arise when Christ is absent.
   "The child Jesus tarried behind in Jerusalem; and Joseph and his mother knew not of it; but they, supposing him to have been in the company, went a day's journey; and they sought him among their kinsfolk and acquaintance. And when they found him not, they turned back again to Jerusalem, seeking him." Luke 2:43-45
2. Life ebbs when Christ is absent.
   "Lord, if thou hadst been here, my brother had not died." John 11:32
3. Storms assail when Christ is absent.
   "He went up into a mountain apart to pray . . . but the ship was now in the midst of the sea, tossed with waves."
   Matt. 14:23, 24
4. Despair prevails when Christ is absent.
   "Except I shall see in his hands the print of the nails, and put my finger into the print of the nails, and put my hand into his side, I will not believe." John 20:25

281. MARY'S MEMORIAL OF DEVOTION

"Mary [took] a pound of ointment of spikenard, very costly, and anointed the feet of Jesus, and wiped his feet with her hair: and the house was filled with the odor of the ointment." John 12:3

1. The extravagance of Mary's devotion.
   a) in the gift of her substance.
   b) in the gift of herself.
2. The "folly" of Mary's devotion.
   a) to humanistic religion.
   John 12:5

109

b) to sinful covetousness.
John 12:6
3. The perception of Mary's devotion.
   a) her devotion perceived the unique work of Christ.
John 12:7
   b) her devotion perceived the unique person of Christ.   John 12:8

—Edmund P. Clowney,
Preaching and Biblical Theology

282. JESUS HAD A FUNERAL

"Let her keep it for the day of my funeral." John 12:7, Goodspeed

In Goodspeed's translation of the New Testament there is a striking rendering of this verse. The familiar version reads as follows: "Let her alone: against the day of my burying hath she kept this." Goodspeed's phrasing of it almost takes our breath away: "Let her alone: let her keep it for the day of my funeral."

"My funeral." How strange and startling these words sound on the lips of the Son of God!

1. Jesus had a funeral—then he is truly and totally human.
2. Jesus had a funeral—then it is no disgrace to occupy a grave.
3. Jesus had a funeral—then the tomb is not the terrible place it once was.
4. Jesus had a funeral—but he also had a resurrection, and for those who love and trust him a glorious future likewise lies in store.

110

283. THE SECRET OF SPIRITUAL FERTILITY

"Verily, verily, I say unto you, Except a corn of wheat fall into the ground and die, it abideth alone: but if it die, it bringeth forth much fruit. John 12:24

1. The immeasurable possibilities of a single life.
   One corn of wheat—much fruit.
2. The irreducible price of a fruitful life.
   It must fall into the ground and die.
3. The infinite pathos of a wasted life.
   The seed not sown abides alone.

—L. E. Deen, quoted by John Woods, *The Preacher's Workshop*

284. THE MAGNETISM OF CHRIST

"And I, if I be lifted up from the earth, will draw all men unto me." John 12:32

We must lift up Christ in:

1. The fullness of his stature.
2. The fullness of his saving power.
3. The fullness of his sacrificial demands.

—Murdo Ewen Macdonald, *The Vitality of Faith*

285. CHRIST DRAWING MEN TO HIMSELF

"I . . . will draw all men unto Me." John 12:32

Why do men need to be drawn to Christ?

1. Because of the distance between man and God.
2. Because of man's inability of himself to come to God.
3. Because of man's disinclination to do so.

286. THE UPLIFTED CHRIST AND UPLIFTED HUMANITY

"And I, when I am lifted up from the earth, will draw all men to myself." John 12:32 RSV

1. Christ uplifted on the cross.
2. The cross uplifting Christ.
3. Christ uplifting the cross.
4. The uplifted Christ through the uplifted cross uplifting humanity.

—B. G. Newton,
Glimpses of God

287. THREE USES OF MONEY

"Then said Jesus unto him [Judas Iscariot], That thou doest, do quickly. Now no man at the table knew for what intent he spake this unto him. For some of them thought, because Judas had the bag, that Jesus had said unto him, Buy those things that we have need of against the feast; or, that he should give something to the poor. He then, having received the sop, went immediately out; and it was night." John 13:27-30

Here we have incidentally brought before us the three uses of money:

1. The purchase of necessities. "Buy those things that we have need of."
2. Disbursement to charities. "Or that he should give something to the poor."
3. All else, in a hungry world like this, is a trading with Christ.
"He went out; and it was night."
"He went his way, and communed with the chief priests and captains, how he might betray unto them. And they were glad, and covenanted to give him money."
Luke 22:4, 5

288. HOMEBUILDING

"I go to prepare a place for you." John 14:2

The instinct of homebuilding is strong in birds, animals, and men. There is in Australia a tiny bird that makes a small garden, plants seeds, and builds a sitting room in which to accommodate its feathered guests. The home building habits of beavers are well known. "They burrow the banks of streams, where they build their houses of timber, twigs and mud. To get timber to their homes they fell trees by gnawing at their base and float them, afterwards constructing dams." And surely among the wonders of the modern world must be reckoned the marvelous houses men and women are building for themselves in our time.

This instinct of home building is a reflection of something in the heart of God himself.

111

Reflect that:

1. He prepared a natural home for us here.
    When we arrived on the scene as babies, we were not exposed to an inhospitable environment. A home had been made ready for us.
2. He has prepared a spiritual home for us in his church. John Henry Newman beautifully said: "The Church is a home for the lonely."
3. He has prepared an eternal home for us in heaven.

289. HEAVEN

"I go to prepare a place for you."
                              John 14:2

1. Heaven is a place.
    "Heaven is to be something rather than to go somewhere."—Canon Farrar
    "Heaven means a state of character rather than a place of residence."
                    —Paterson Smyth
2. Heaven is a prepared place.
    a) It is prepared big enough.
    b) Heaven is full of beauty.
    c) Heaven is a comfortable place.
3. Heaven is a busy place.
4. Heaven is a place of communion and social activity.
5. Heaven is an eternal place.
    Someone has said that when we get to heaven there will be three surprises. First, to see some people we did not expect to see. Second, not to see some people we did expect to see. And third, the greatest surprise of all, will be to find ourselves there.
                              —Unknown

290. THE SECOND COMING

"I will come again, and receive you unto myself."   John 14:3

1. The Son of God came once.
2. He who came once will come again.
3. His coming will be to receive you unto himself.

                    —James Dinwoodie,
        Illustrated Sermon Outlines

291. THE LORD'S RETURN

"I will come again, and receive you unto myself."   John 14:3

1. The Lord will certainly return.
2. We cannot possibly find out when.
3. Therefore we should always be ready for him.

                              —C. S. Lewis

292. CHRIST—THE CENTER

"I am the way, the truth, and the life."   John 14:6

Christ here proclaims his own centrality.

1. Christ is the center from whom the way radiates.
2. Christ is the center from whom the truth emanates.
3. Christ is the center from whom the life operates.

293. VIA, VERITAS, VITA

"I am the way, the truth, and the life."   John 14:6

1. Without the way, there is no going.
2. Without the truth, there is no knowing.

3. Without the life, there is no growing.

—Unknown

294. THE CHRIST OF EVERY ROAD

"I am the way." John 14:6

1. The Christ of the Galilean Road.
   The burdened heart of service.
2. The Christ of the Calvary Road.
   The broken heart of sacrifice.
3. The Christ of the Emmaus Road.
   The burning heart of evangelism.

—A. C. Holt,
in *Snappy Sermon Starters*

295. CHRIST—THE WAY

"I am the way." John 14:6

1. Christ is the way *in*.
   Salvation.
2. Christ is the way *out*.
   Service.
3. Christ is the way *up*.
   Sanctification.

—Unknown

296. CHRIST'S THREE GREAT PROMISES

"I will pray the Father, and he shall give you another Comforter."
John 14:16
"I will build my church."
Matt. 16:18
"I will come again." John 14:3

1. The promise of the Comforter.
2. The promise of the Community.
3. The promise of the Coming.

297. THE WORLD'S THREE GREATEST EVENTS

"Yet a little while, and the world seeth me no more; but ye see me: because I live, ye shall live also."
John 14:19

1. "A little while, and the world seeth me no more."
   That is Good Friday.
2. "But ye see me."
   That is Easter Sunday.
3. "Because I live, ye shall live also."
   That is Pentecost.

—Tom Rees,
The Spirit of Life

298. THE THREE CHOICES

"Ye have not chosen me, but I have chosen you, and ordained you, that ye should go and bring forth fruit, and that your fruit should remain. John 15:16

All life is a series of choices. Some are unimportant, like choosing a tie or a frock. Some are serious, like the choice of a profession. Some are vital, where the choice lies between good and evil, between right and wrong. Every choice, even the unimportant ones, goes to the building of character. If I may add one stage to the old adage, it is just as true:

Sow a Thought, and you reap an Act;
Sow an Act, and you reap a Habit;
Sow a Habit, and you reap a Character;
Sow a Character, and you reap a Destiny.

Think of the three choices referred to in the text:

1. Man's choice of Christ.
   "Ye have not chosen me."

2. Christ's choice of man.
"I have chosen you."
3. Christ's choice for men.
"And ordained you, that ye should go and bring forth fruit, and that your fruit should remain."

JOHN 16–21

299. THE INSPIRING SPIRIT

"Howbeit when he, the Spirit of truth, is come, he will guide you into all truth . . . he will shew you things to come. He shall glorify me." John 16:13, 14

Christ here sets predictively before his disciples the role of the Holy Spirit in the inspiration of the New Testament.

1. He shall glorify me.
   That is the Spirit inspiring the writing of the Gospels.
2. He will guide you into all truth.
   That is the Spirit inspiring the authors of the Epistles.
3. He will show you things to come.
   That is the Spirit inspiring the composition of the Book of Revelation.

—Unknown

300. THE ALONENESS OF CHRIST

"Ye shall be scattered, every man to his own, and shall leave me alone: and yet I am not alone, because the Father is with me." John 16:32

Jesus was at times alone, but he was not lonely. There is a difference between aloneness and loneliness.

Loneliness is a mood of the spirit: aloneness is a matter of environment. Like another, but with infinitely more meaning, he could say: "Never less alone than when alone." "Ye shall leave me alone, yet I am not alone."

Think of the aloneness of Christ in five directions:

1. He was alone in the severity of his temptations.
2. He was alone in the privacy of his prayers.
3. He was alone in the supremacy of his thought.
4. He was alone in the sublimity of his sacrifice.
5. He was alone in the secrecy of his resurrection.

And all alone, alone, alone
He rose again behind the stone.
—Alice Meynell

301. WHY CHRISTIANS MUST GO ON LIVING IN THE WORLD

"I pray not that thou shouldest take them out of the world." John 17:15

A little girl once said to her mother: "If God wants to get us all to heaven at last, why doesn't he take us there right away?"

114

It was a fair question.
What is the answer to it?
Jesus provides three replies to
it in this chapter.

1. We need to remain in the
   world for our own sakes.
   "Sanctify them through thy
   truth."   John 17:17
2. We need to remain in the
   world for the world's sake.
   "I [have] sent them into the
   world."   John 17:18
3. We need to remain in the
   world for God's sake.
   "That the world may believe
   that thou hast sent me."

John 17:21

—William H. Young,
How to Preach With Power
(adapted)

302. CHRIST—MAKING THE MOST OF HIMSELF

"I make the most of myself."
John 17:19a (trans. suggested
by A. W. Blackwood)

Note that:

1. Christ made the most of himself as carpenter.
2. Christ made the most of himself as teacher.
3. Christ made the most of himself as Savior.

303. THE CUP

"The cup which my Father hath given me, shall I not drink it?"
John 18:11

With trembling reverence I
have taken into my hands on
several occasions what must be the
most famous communion cups in
Wales. One is made of pewter, another of silver, and the third of old
blackened and broken wood. The
pewter cup is at Llangeitho. It was
the sacramental chalice used by
Daniel Rowland at the great communion services of the revival there.
The silver cup is at Trevecca. It belonged to Howell Harris and was
employed at the celebration of the
Lord's Supper during the spiritual
awakening in that locality. The
third and wooden cup is in the ancient, rambling mansion of Nanteos, near Aberystwyth, and is alleged to be the Holy Grail itself. To
anyone with a vivid historical
imagination, merely to hold these
cups in one's hands is a never-to-be-forgotten experience.

We are not told of what material
the cup was made from which our
Lord and his disciples drank on
the night of the betrayal. But, after
all, does that matter? It is not the
composition but the content of the
cup that is significant.

Note that:

1. It was God who gave the cup.

There is a grand story of Alexander
the Great's confidence in his friend
and physician. When the physician had
mixed him a potion for his sickness, a
letter was put into Alexander's hand,
warning him not to drink the mixture
because it was poisoned. He held the
letter in the one hand and the cup in
the other, and in the presence of his
friend and physician he drank up the
draught; and, after he had drained the
cup, he bade his friend look at that
letter and judge of his confidence in
him. Alexander had unstaggering faith
in his friend, which did not admit of
doubt. "See now," said he, "how I

115

have trusted you." This is the assurance which the believer should exercise towards his God.

—Charles Haddon Spurgeon

2. It was guilt that filled the cup.

I wonder if you have read in Plato's *Phaedo* the deeply moving account of the death of Socrates. Socrates who, it is said, had "never done any wicked thing," was sentenced to death by his Athenian judges. He was to die by poisoning. A cup was filled with hemlock and handed to him. As he raised it to his lips, the philosopher spoke to his disciples about death and immortality. Then he quaffed the fatal draught. Bit by bit he felt a cold deadness creeping over his body from the feet upwards, mounting towards his heart. And suddenly, wrapping his face in his mantle, he expired, and so passed from this world one of its greatest men.

But there was a bitterer and more lethal draught than that, and it was given to an infinitely better person than Socrates. It was the cup of human sin and it was handed to Jesus Christ. He drank it to the dregs. As Anne Ross Cousin wrote:

Death and the curse were in our cup,
O Christ, 'twas full for Thee!
But Thou hast drained the last dark drop,
'Tis empty now for me:
That bitter cup,
Love drank it up,
Now blessing's draught for me.

116

3. It is grace that flows from the cup.

Someone has beautifully written: "Cleopatra put a jewel in a cup, which contained the price of a kingdom. This sacred cup we are to drink of, enriched with the blood of God, is above the price of a kingdom."

304. THE TRUTH AND MEN

"Every one that is of the truth heareth my voice." John 18:37

Men must be led:

1. To learn the truth.
   To acknowledge it.
2. To love the truth.
   To approve it.
3. To live the truth.
   To act it in daily life.

—E. Tyrrell Green,
How to Preach

305. TETELESTAI

"It is finished." John 19:30

What was finished? We will try to answer the question from Christ's own words—more particularly from three picture-phrases which he himself used.

1. Christ saw his passion and death as a cup to be drunk. "Let this cup pass from me." Matt. 26:39
2. Christ saw his passion as a road to be traveled. "The Son of man indeed goeth, as it is written of him." Mark 14:21
3. Christ saw his passion as a price to be paid. "The Son of man came not

to be ministered unto, but to minister, and to give his life a ransom for many."
Matt. 20:28

—A. M. Hunter, *Teaching and Preaching the New Testament*

306. FINISHED

"It is finished." John 19:30

There is always a peculiar satisfaction in finishing a piece of work. It may be the building of a house, the writing of a book, the construction of a great machine. Whatever it is, its completion brings to the one employed on it a gratifying sense of accomplishment. At last he is able to say: "I have finished the work."

Some people, it has to be recognized, never finish anything. They lack the qualities of persistence and perseverance, and their lives are littered with jobs half done and aims half realized. Beginning an enterprise with boundless enthusiasm, they soon lose taste for it and set it aside unfinished.

Others fail to finish their work because death robs them of the opportunity. Before they have a chance to achieve their purposes or carry their plans to fruition, their lives are cut short. Think of Matthew Henry and his monumental *Commentary*. He died after completing his notes on Matthew's Gospel, and other hands had to finish what he had begun. Or think of Schubert with his famous "Unfinished Symphony," a musical inspiration which he never managed fully to work out. Or think of Cecil Rhodes with his dream of the development of Africa and the Cape to Cairo Railway, dying before his schemes could materialize with the wistful lament: "So much to do, so little done!"

Jesus completed the colossal task assigned to him, despite the brevity of his earthly career. On the Cross he was able to cry: "It is finished!" In this, as in all other things, he is our example. Let us see to it that we, too, by his grace and in his strength seek to complete the work committed to us. Observe that:

1. Every man must have a master.
   Thomas Carlyle once said that a man's first duty is to find his work. Someone has corrected that with the retort: "No, a man's first duty is to find his master."
2. To every man that master will assign a task.
   Note:
   a) Some do no work.
   b) Some only do enough work to gag their conscience.
   c) Some work for the love of it.
   d) Some work because they are conscious that God has given them a job to do.
3. Happy is the man who, at the close of his life, can honestly claim to have finished the labor to which he was divinely directed.

307. THE SECRET DISCIPLE

"Joseph of Arimathea, being a disciple of Jesus, but secretly for fear

117

of the Jews, besought Pilate that he might take away the body of Jesus." John 19:38

Our text is suggestive of certain practical considerations:

1. Good men may be found in unlikely places.
2. Good men are sometimes found in false positions.
3. Good men are sometimes dominated by wrong forces.
4. Great occasions reveal latent qualities of goodness.

—Mark Brokenshire,
The Veiled Tomorrow

308. THE FOLDED NAPKIN

"The napkin, that was about his head, not lying with the linen clothes, but wrapped together in a place by itself." John 20:7

Here we have an illustration of:

1. Christ's love of order.
   "Wrapped . . . in a place by itself."
2. Christ's care of the property of others.
   The napkin was borrowed.
3. Christ's unhurried calm.
   He was rising from the dead —the most stupendous thing he ever did—but he took time to leave the tomb tidy. This speaks of self-possession.
4. Christ's delight in personal service.
   He folded the napkin. The napkin, like the towel, was a symbol of his lowly willingness to minister.

—B. D. Johns,
Pulpit Notes

309. THE UPPER ROOM

John 20:19-29

Consider in what condition the risen Christ found his disciples in the Upper Room and what benefits he conferred upon them.

1. They were terrified.
   He gave them his peace.
   "The doors were shut . . . for fear . . . Jesus . . . saith, Peace be unto you."
   John 20:19
2. They were mystified.
   He gave them his presence.
3. They were mortified.
   He gave them his pardon.
4. They were stultified.
   He gave them his power.

310. THEN JESUS CAME

"Then the same day at evening, being the first day of the week, when the doors were shut where the disciples were assembled for fear of the Jews, came Jesus and stood in the midst, and saith unto them, Peace be unto you."
John 20:19

1. He comes in a time of crisis.
2. He comes in unexpected ways and at unlikely times.
3. He comes through closed doors.

311. THE HANDS OF JESUS

"He showed unto them his hands."
John 20:20

What a wonderful thing is the human hand! Thomas Chalmers, the great Scottish churchman, wrote of the human hand: "It contains more evidence of divine

118

purpose than that of the movement of a planet in its orbit."

Look for a little at the hands of Jesus.

Note that they are:

1. The horny hands of toil.
The life of our Lord was not, as we say, "a lord's life." It was the life of a workingman. Says James Russell Lowell:

No man is born into the world whose work
Is not born with him; there is always work,
And tools to work withal, for those who will;
And blessèd are the horny hands of toil!

2. The hallowing hands of love. "Then were there brought unto him [Jesus] little children, that he should put his hands on them, and pray." Matt. 19:13
3. The healing hands of pity. "Now when the sun was setting, all they that had any sick with divers diseases brought them unto him [Jesus]; and he laid his hands on every one of them, and healed them." Luke 4:40
4. The helping hands of power. "Immediately Jesus stretched forth his hand, and caught him [Peter]." Matt. 14:31

"All my life," confessed Seneca, the Roman philosopher, "I have been seeking to climb out of the rut of my besetting sins. And I can't do it; and I never will, unless a hand is let down to draw me up."

"Faith, really," as Harold Brierley succinctly put it, "is

holding out your hand in the dark, and finding it held."

5. The holed hands of sacrifice. "He showed unto them his hands." John 20:20

312. SHUT DOORS

"Then came Jesus, the doors being shut, and stood in the midst, and said, Peace be unto you."
John 20:26

1. The door of the room was shut.
2. The doors of some minds present were shut.
3. No door can keep Christ from coming to his own.

—James Dinwoodie,
Illustrated Sermon Outlines

313. THE NEXT MORNING

"When the morning was now come, Jesus stood on the shore."
John 21:4

Some of you may recall that last, poignant entry in the diary of Sir Walter Scott: "We slept reasonably, but on the next morning—!" Death broke off the sentence. "The next morning." What is that to be?

1. Some deny that there is to be a next morning.
"I believe," wrote Bertrand Russell, "that when I die I shall rot, and that nothing of my ego shall survive."
2. Some doubt whether or not there will be a next morning.
"We do not see enough," affirmed James Paget, "to form a final conclusion from what we see here."

119

3. Some declare their faith in a next morning.

Said Charles Kingsley: "I look forward to death with intense, reverent curiosity." One of the most moving sermons I ever read on the afterlife was the product of an old preacher who took as text: "When the morning was now come, Jesus stood on the shore."

314. THE LOGIC OF GRACE

Hegel, the great German philosopher, maintained that all logical thought proceeds through three stages—a yes, a no, and a nevertheless.

In the New Testament we may trace three such responses to the Divine. The speaker on each occasion is Simon Peter.

1. Yes, Lord.
   "Yea, Lord; thou knowest that I love thee."
   John 21:15, 16
2. No, Lord.
   "Not so, Lord; for I have never. . . ."   Acts 10:14
3. Nevertheless, Lord.
   "Nevertheless at thy word I will let down the net."
   Luke 5:5

ACTS

315. THE CHARIOT OF CLOUD

"*A cloud received him out of their sight.*"   Acts 1:9

This cloud signified:

1. Separation.
   Christ vanished, and the disciples had only a cloud left upon which to fix their gaze.
2. Revelation.
   While the cloud concealed Christ from their natural vision, it revealed him to their spiritual vision. No longer could they doubt the deity of their master.
3. Mutation.
   Clouds change and disappear. Jesus had assured his disciples that he must be separated from them for a season that he might prepare a place for them in heaven.
4. Exaltation.
   Christ had mounted in triumph to a throne. He had not just vanished into thin air. He had ascended from the earth as a cloud ascends, to be transfigured in heaven.

—John Mitchell, *Shot and Shell for a Preacher's Gun*

316. GREAT PRAYER MEETINGS IN THE BOOK OF ACTS

(A Prayer Meeting Sermon)

1. The prayer meeting that brought the power down.
   "These all continued with one accord in prayer . . .

with the women, and Mary the mother of Jesus, and with his brethren."

Acts 1:14

2. The prayer meeting that brought the apostle out.

"Peter therefore was kept in prison: but prayer was made without ceasing of the church unto God for him."

Acts 12:5

3. The prayer meeting that let the gospel in.

"On the sabbath we went out of the city by a river side, where prayer was wont to be made; and we sat down, and spake unto the women which were resorted thither."

Acts 16:13

317. THE BOOK OF ONE ACCORD

With one accord: note recurrence of this phrase in Acts.

1. Unity of purpose.

Acts 1:14

2. Unity of prayer. Acts 2:1
3. Unity of place.   Acts 2:46
4. Unity of power. Acts 5:12
5. Unity of proclamation.

Acts 8:6

6. Unity of propagation.

Acts 15:25

318. PENTECOST

"When the day of Pentecost was fully come."   Acts 2:1

Observe that:

1. Pentecost is factual, not fictional.
2. Pentecost is spiritual, not just psychological.

3. Pentecost is moral, not merely emotional.
4. Pentecost is communal, not only individual.
5. Pentecost is perpetual, not ephemeral.

319. THREE RESPONSES TO PENTECOST

Acts 2:1-18

The spectacular phenomena of the day of Pentecost called forth from those who observed them three revealing responses.

Pentecost does so still.

Let us note briefly what those responses are:

1. The response of bewilderment.

"What on earth can this mean?" Acts 2:12 Phillips

2. The response of disparagement.

"These men are full of new wine."   Acts 2:13

3. The response of discernment.

"This is that." Acts 2:16

320. FILLED WITH THE HOLY GHOST

"And they were all filled with the Holy Ghost."   Acts 2:4

It will do us a great deal of good to look at these people to whom the Holy Spirit was given on the day of Pentecost.

Note that they were:

1. Simple folk.

I use the word "simple" in the sense of ordinary. When we look down the list we find no distinguished people. As one writer has put it: "I

121

look through this list and I cannot find in it the name of a single nobleman; I cannot find in it the name of a single rabbi; I cannot find in it the name of a single honourable councillor; I cannot find in it the name of a single man of wealth or position. What I do find are fishermen and publicans and quondam outlaws."

2. Sinful folk.
Among them was Peter, who had denied his Lord; James and John were there—they who had been filled with wrong ambition; others were there who had been social outcasts.

3. Seeking folk.
"They were all with one accord in one place." Acts 2:1
"These all continued with one accord in prayer and supplication." Acts 1:14

—J. Ithel Jones,
Temple and Town

321. INTOXICATION

"For these are not drunken, as ye suppose, seeing it is but the third hour of the day." Acts 2:15

It is very significant that when these early Christians were let loose upon the world on that first Whitsun, the people looking on thought they were drunk.

What signs of drunkenness are to be seen in these Spirit-filled people?

1. They have loosened tongues.
One of the early and sure signs of intoxication is that people start talking freely. So here!

2. They have a sense of being on good terms with everything and everybody.
To the intoxicated man everything in the garden is lovely.

3. They are hilarious, irrepressibly gleeful.
They were Christ's "Laughing Cavaliers."

—J. Ithel Jones,
Temple and Town

322. SPIRITUAL ARITHMETIC

(As exemplified in the life of the early church)

1. Addition.
Three thousand added.
Acts 2:41

2. Subtraction.
Two taken away, Ananias and Sapphira. Acts 5:1-10

3. Multiplication.
Disciples multiplied.
Acts 6:1

4. Division.
Believers scattered abroad.
Acts 8:1

—George W. Noble,
750 Sermon Outlines

323. WHAT REPENTANCE BRINGS

"Repent therefore, and turn again, that your sins may be blotted out, that times of refreshing may come from the presence of the Lord, and that he may send the Christ appointed for you, Jesus."
Acts 3:19, 20 RSV

Here we see repentance related to:

1. The remission of sins.
   "That your sins may be blotted out."
2. The refreshing of revival.
   "So there may come seasons of refreshing."
3. The return of the Lord.
   "That he may send the Christ."

324. THE IRREPRESSIBLE IN CHRISTIAN CONVICTION

"We cannot but speak."

Acts 4:20

There are some things we cannot help doing.

Let us consider one or two of them together.

1. Automatic physical reflexes.

Professor Stout quotes the example of a soldier secretly storming a height in the dark. He feels a tickling in the nose, but decides not to sneeze. All the grounds of his own safety, his children, his comrades, the success of the venture, devotion to his general, his country, his duty—all these desires create a powerful dominant "universe"; but he knows he is going to sneeze, and finally does so.

—Edgar R. Jones

2. External compulsion.
   When a couple of stalwart constables pinion a small man by the arms and ask him to accompany them to the local police station, he can hardly help going!
3. Irrepressible Christian conviction.
   There is that about Christian truth which lays upon him

who grasps it the irresistible onus of communicating it to others. Peter felt that urge when he declared: "We cannot but speak."

325. THE WORD PETER NEVER USED

"Whom ye slew and hanged on a tree."

Acts 5:30

"Who his own self bare our sins in his own body on the tree."

I Pet. 2:24

Psychologists are familiar with the fact that when some particular word has for us painful or unpleasant associations we tend to stumble over it or to omit it from conversation. Such verbal inhibitions in their patients provide psychoanalysts with valuable clues in their efforts to diagnose mental maladies.

In the Apostle Peter's vocabulary there would seem to have been such a word. It was the word "Cross." Peter could never bring himself to say it. You will search his recorded speeches in the Book of Acts and his two epistles in vain for the term. It just is not there. When placed under the necessity of using it, the apostle took refuge in euphemism. He substituted for it the word "tree."

Or perhaps Peter did so because he preferred the word "tree!" There is certainly something highly suggestive in his appropriation of the term for this purpose.

Consider that:

1. A tree is a beautiful thing.
2. A tree is a useful thing.
   From its timber so many articles can be made.

123

3. A tree is an enduring thing. The oldest living things in the world are trees.

326. PREACHING CHRIST

"Philip went down to the city of Samaria, and preached Christ unto them." Acts 8:5

We ought to have the same message. We ought to:

1. Preach Christ—nothing less!
2. Preach Christ—nothing more!
3. Preach Christ—nothing else!

327. GUIDED OR GOADED?

"It is hard for thee to kick against the goads." Acts 9:5

There is the clear ring of truth about these recorded words of the risen Christ. They do not appear in some of the oldest manuscripts of the New Testament, and so have been omitted from the Revised Standard Version.

All the same, we may be sure that Jesus spoke them. They sound like Jesus. The figure is agricultural, the sort of metaphor which the Master commonly employed.

And what it comes to is this: Some people will not be guided and so have to be goaded.

Note certain points of difference between them:

1. Goading is external; guiding is internal.
   Benjamin Warfield speaks about divine guidance being "transferred from external compulsion to internal influence."

2. Goading is compulsive; guiding is cooperative.
   When God goads us he urges us on against our will; when he guides us he directs and energizes our will.
3. Goading is painful; guiding is pleasurable.
   There are times when, lost in a trackless desert, the most pleasant experience one can have is to be guided.

328. THE IDEAL CHURCH FOR TODAY

"Many . . . were come together." Acts 10:27 ff.

The passage Acts 10:24-48 suggests as an ideal for today a local church with:

1. A minister like Peter. Acts 10:24-29
   a) Responds to the call of God.
   b) Follows the guidance of the Spirit.
   c) Shows a new feeling of humility.
2. Lay leaders like Cornelius. Acts 10:30-33a
   a) Men who pray before they act.
   b) Men who give as freely as they pray.
   c) Men who live in the spirit of faith.
3. People like those in Caesarea. Acts 10:33b-48
   a) Come to church on time.
   b) Hear the Word of God gladly.
   c) Receive the Holy Spirit.

—Andrew W. Blackwood, *Expository Preaching for Today*

329. THE IDEAL CONGREGATION

"Now therefore are we all here present before God, to hear all things that are commanded thee of God." Acts 10:33

Here we have presented to us the ideal congregation. Note its characteristics:

1. It was punctual.
   "Now therefore we are all here."
2. It was reverent.
   "Present before God."
3. It was attentive.
   "To hear all things that are commanded thee of God."

—B. D. Johns, *Pulpit Notes*

330. WHAT IS A CHRISTIAN?

"The disciples were called Christians first in Antioch." Acts 11:26

What is a Christian? No noun in the language so urgently needs exact definition. Some claim the title who have no right to it, and others to whom the name would willingly be given by all thoughtful and observant people, disclaim it altogether, professing themselves utterly unworthy of it. "I die a Christian," said Casanova, one of the greatest profligates of history. "I am not a Christian," cried John Wesley, one of the greatest saints of history.

What an anomaly! The rake professes himself a Christian: the revivalist modestly abjures the honor.

What, then, is a Christian? Let us note, first, what a Christian is not:
a) A Christian is not just one who has been born in a Christian country or community.
b) A Christian is not merely one who has been christened in a Christian church.
c) A Christian is not simply one who gives intellectual assent to a creed.
d) A Christian is not just one who attempts to regulate his life in accordance with the ethic of Jesus.
e) A Christian is not merely one who has his name inscribed on a church register.

What, then, is a Christian? Let me offer three answers to the question.

1. A Christian is one who believes something about Jesus.
   a) that he is God as well as man.
   b) that he died for our sins and is our only Savior.
   c) that he is alive and offers us his friendship.
   d) that he is the destined Judge and Ruler of mankind.
2. A Christian is one who receives something from Jesus. In his spiritual autobiography, *What Christianity Means to Me*, Lyman Beecher wrote:

"As far back as I remember I always wished to be a Christian. But I curiously failed to understand what the Christian life is. It was not until at about eighteen years of age I came under the influence of Henry Ward Beecher's preaching that I began to understand that Jesus is not a lawgiver but a life-giver, and that one is not a Christian because he obeys the laws of God, but he obeys the laws of God because he is a Christian."

3. A Christian is one who achieves something for Jesus. Of William Ewart Gladstone, John Morley, his biographer, memorably said: "Gladstone was not a Christian for nothing."

331. NEW TESTAMENT NAMES FOR CHRISTIANS

"And the disciples were called Christians first in Antioch."
Acts 11:26

1. They were known as disciples. "He called unto him his twelve disciples."
Matt. 10:1
2. They were known as believers. "Believers were the more added to the Lord."
Acts 5:14
3. They were known as brethren. "Behold . . . my brethren."
Matt. 12:49
4. They were known as saints. "The saints salute you."
Phil. 4:22
Thus: knowledge, faith, love, and holiness were their distinguishing characteristics.

—James Dinwoodie, *Illustrated Sermon Outlines*

332. WHAT IS A CHRISTIAN?

"The disciples were called Christians first in Antioch."
Acts 11:26

Let us try to supply three answers to that question.

1. A Christian is one who shares the life of Christ.
2. A Christian is one who keeps the law of Christ.
3. A Christian is one who bears the likeness of Christ.

333. SERVING ONE'S GENERATION

"David, after he had served his own generation by the will of God, fell on sleep." Acts 13:36

1. Those who serve their own age, serve every age, for there is a glorious continuity in all time.
2. Those who serve their own generation by the will of God serve what is really paramount and permanent in all the story of time.
3. Those who serve their own generation and "fall on sleep" fulfill a threefold ministry.
   a) in the institutions they helped to found.
   b) in the inspirations they still create.
   c) in the service they still render before God's face.

—Andrew Fairbairn, in *Some Reminiscences and Studies*

334. THE DOOR OF FAITH

"He had opened the door of faith."
Acts 14:27

1. Shall the door remain unopened?
2. Shall the door open inwards?

3. Shall the door open outwards?

—H. A. Hammerton, in
Expository Times

335. THE NOBLE BEREANS

"They . . . searched the Scriptures
daily, whether these things were
so." Acts 17:11

There are different ways of reading
the Bible.

1. Some read it for argument's
sake.
So as to be able to debate
about it.
2. Some read it for advance-
ment's sake.
So as to improve their own
minds.
3. Some read it for attach-
ment's sake.
Out of love for the Lord.

336. JESUS IS OUR JUDGE

"He [God] hath appointed a day,
in the which he will judge the
world in righteousness by that man
whom he hath ordained."
Acts 17:31

In his brilliant monograph on
Alexander Whyte, John Kelman
relates that when Whyte spoke in
the pulpit in awed tones of sin
and its indictment at the bar of
God: "We were afraid as we looked
on him, and when after some terrific denunciation he would shut
his mouth and look abroad on the
people, every one of us felt as if it
were the Day of Judgement."

Every day we meet Jesus is a Day
of Judgment.

1. We are always judged by the
best.
2. Jesus is the best we know.
3. He judges us now:
   a) by what he said when on
   earth.
   b) by the record of what he
   was when on earth.
   c) by what he is in our
   hearts.
   d) by what we see of him
   in the lives of others.
4. By him we shall be judged
at last.

Oh, may we stand before the Lamb,
When earth and seas are fled,
And hear the Judge pronounce our
name
With blessings on our head!
—From The Scottish Psalter

337. FOUR HUMAN TYPES

"Gallio cared for none of those
things." Acts 18:17
"All the Athenians, and strangers
which were there, spent their time
in nothing else, but either to tell,
or to hear some new thing."
Acts 17:21
"These that . . . turned the world
upside down." Acts 17:6
"Behold, I make all things new."
Rev. 21:5

1. The spectators.
Ernest Renan wrote: "How
ungrateful I should be if I
grumbled at my lot! For
sixty-four years I have been
a spectator of this admirable
show—the universe; I have
had a comfortable arm-chair
and footstool, and I have
watched the world at one of
the most interesting moments
of its development."

127

"Though the most be players," said Ben Jonson, "some must be spectators." Gallio was such.

2. The commentators.
The Athenians were such. To them life was not a conflict but a subject for interminable commentary.

3. The agitators.
Paul and Silas were such. Of them it was said that "they turned the world upside down." That text provided the quaint old preacher with three pithy points:
a) The world is the wrong way up.
b) It must be got the right way up.
c) We are the boys to do it!

4. The regenerator.
It has been said: "Some men are crying out 'Agitate!' others are crying out 'Legislate!' but the cry which the world needs is 'Regenerate!' " Jesus is the great Regenerator. "Behold," he says, "I make all things new." As George Matheson pointed out, that is not the same as making new things. Christ takes the old and makes it new.

338. THE CHURCH WHICH HAD NEVER HEARD OF THE HOLY GHOST!

"We have not so much as heard whether there be any Holy Ghost."
Acts 19:2

Here is the strangest confession on record. It is as if men living in the middle of the Sahara Desert should profess never to have heard

of the sun, or people stranded on a Pacific island should declare that they had never heard of the sea!

For consider:

1. This was a church which had listened to the eloquent exposition of the Scriptures.
Yet it had not heard of the Holy Ghost!
"And a certain Jew named Apollos, born at Alexandria, an eloquent man, and mighty in the Scriptures, came to Ephesus. . . . And he began to speak boldly in the synagogue."   Acts 18:24-26

2. This was a church which practiced the ceremonial rites of religion.
Yet it had not heard of the Holy Ghost!
"He [Paul] said unto them, Unto what then were ye baptized? And they said, Unto John's baptism." Acts 19:3

3. This was a church which had experienced the delights of Christian fellowship.
Yet it had not heard of the Holy Ghost!
"All the men were about twelve."   Acts 19:7

4. This was a church living in the pentecostal era.
Yet it had not heard of the Holy Ghost!
"The Holy Ghost came on them."   Acts 19:6

How many churches are like that today!

339. SLAVE AND FREE

"I was free-born." Acts 22:28
"Paul, a bond-slave of Jesus Christ."   Rom. 1:1

128

We see here:

1. A freeman who was nevertheless a slave.

The population of Rome during the first century of the Christian era was 1,610,000 and of that number 900,000 were slaves. Think of it—three out of five of the men and women whom Paul passed on the streets of the imperial city were slaves, with less rights in the eyes of the law than your dog.
—George Jackson

2. A slave who was nevertheless a free man.

"How much for this old slave?" cried a glib auctioneer in the dark slavery days. "25 dollars! Only 25 dollars for this fine old man! 30 is bid, 40, 50—do I hear 50? 60! 65! Any advance upon 65 dollars?" The old Negro's heart beat quick and his eyes filled with tears. He had somehow managed to save a little money, hoping to buy himself free; but the bids were running up beyond his means. At last, in a voice with a tear trembling in it, he cried out: "70 dollars!" The slave-buyers stood aghast; they had no heart to make another bid; in fact, the whole crowd was half-paralyzed. "70! 70!" exclaimed the auctioneer. "Any advance on 70? Going! Going! Gone!" Down went the hammer, and the next instant the old slave leapt into liberty. He was able to purchase his freedom, but the sinner cannot do so.

3. How it happened.
Christ took the free man [Paul] and made him a slave, and he took the slave [Paul] and made him a free man.
"In giving freedom to the slave," said Abraham Lincoln, "we assure freedom to the free—honorable alike in what we give and in what we preserve."

"It is told that Abraham Lincoln in a slave-market saw a girl being sold," writes William Barclay.

He was so sorry for her that he himself bought her and then handed her her papers of freedom. When she took them, she said: Am I free now? "Yes," he said. "Free," she asked, "to go anywhere I like?" "Yes," he said. "Then," she cried, "I will follow you for the rest of my life!"

That is what happened to Paul. His was the prayer which George Matheson put into imperishable words:

Make me a captive, Lord,
And then I shall be free.

340. THE VOICE THAT QUIETS YOUR FEARS

"Fear not, Paul . . . God hath given thee all them that sail with thee." Acts 27:24

In every storm of life the Lord stands by to help.

1. He may permit you to enter into peril.
2. He enables you to conquer every fear.
3. He fills you with concern for persons in distress.
It is evident from the text that Paul's fears were not for himself, but for his fellow passengers.

—Andrew W. Blackwood,
Doctrinal Preaching for Today

129

ROMANS

341. THE RESURRECTION IN ROMANS

"Jesus Christ . . . declared to be the Son of God with power . . . by the resurrection from the dead." Rom. 1:3-4

"[Christ was] raised again for our justification." Rom. 4:25

"If the Spirit of him that raised up Jesus from the dead dwell in you, he that raised up Christ from the dead shall also quicken your mortal bodies by his Spirit that dwelleth in you." Rom. 8:11

1. The Resurrection verifies Christ's claims.
   "Declared to be the Son of God . . . by the resurrection."
2. The Resurrection justifies the repentant sinner.
   "Raised . . . for our justification."
3. The Resurrection vivifies the saint.
   "He that raised up Christ . . . shall also quicken your mortal bodies."

342. READINESS IS ALL

"I am ready to preach the gospel to you that are at Rome also." Rom. 1:15

"I am ready to come to you." II Cor. 12:14

"I am now ready to be offered." II Tim. 4:6

Here we see Paul:
1. Eager to preach Christ.
2. Eager to forgive in Christ.
3. Eager to die for Christ.

—A. Skevington Wood,
Heralds of the Gospel

343. A GOSPEL TO BE PROUD OF

"I am not ashamed of the gospel of Christ." Rom. 1:16

1. It is a gospel of sanity.
2. It is a gospel of simplicity.
3. It is a gospel of security.

—Murdo Ewen Macdonald,
The Vitality of Faith

344. WHAT PAUL WAS NOT ASHAMED OF

"I am not ashamed of the gospel of Christ: for it is the power of God unto salvation to every one that believeth." Rom. 1:16

There were many things that Paul might have been ashamed of. He was a Jew, and he might have been ashamed of belonging to that despised race. He was a dwarf, measuring, according to one tradition, a bare four feet six, and he might have been ashamed of being diminutive. He was poor, having hardly a penny to bless himself with, and he might have been ashamed of being poor. But there was one thing of which Paul could never be ashamed—the gospel of Christ!

In our text he tells us why:
1. Because of its content.
   "It is the power of God."
   The gospel is power, and nobody is ever ashamed of power.
2. Because of its concern.
   "To every one."
   The gospel is for all.

3. Because of its condition.
"That believeth."
Its sole condition is simple faith.

345. THE USEFULNESS OF CHRISTIANITY

"[The gospel] is the power of God unto salvation." Rom. 1:16

"Christianity is nothing," it has been pointedly said, "if it is of no use to us." Ours is a markedly utilitarian age in which things have to prove their worth by showing that they work. Modern men are not interested in anything that is not practicable.

Is Christianity practicable? Is it useful?

I suggest that it is:

1. It is useful to an alarmed conscience.
2. It is useful to a distracted mind.
3. It is useful to a broken heart.
4. It is useful to a war-fearing world.
   The world today is war-fearing when it is not warfaring.

346. THE THEREFORES IN ROMANS

Someone has wisely and wittily said that in reading Romans we ought to look out for the "therefores" and see what they are there for!

He was right. The word "therefore" is indeed a key word to the understanding of the profound epistle.

Let us, then, look for a little at the therefores.

1. The therefore of accusation.
   "Therefore thou art inex-cusable, O man, whosoever thou art that judgest: for wherein thou judgest another, thou condemnest thyself." Rom. 2:1
2. The therefore of justification.
   "Therefore being justified by faith, we have peace with God through our Lord Jesus Christ." Rom. 5:1
   "God," wrote Richard Hooker, "doth justify the believing man, yet not for the worthiness of his belief, but for the worthiness of Him which is believed."
3. The therefore of identification.
   "Therefore we are buried with him by baptism into death; that like as Christ was raised up from the dead by the glory of the Father, even so we also should walk in newness of life." Rom. 6:4
4. The therefore of sanctification.
   "There is therefore now no condemnation to them which are in Christ Jesus." Rom. 8:1
5. The therefore of consecration.
   "I beseech you therefore, brethren, by the mercies of God, that ye present your bodies a living sacrifice, holy, acceptable unto God, which is your reasonable service." Rom. 12:1
   God meets man at the point of sacrifice. That is the dominant truth of the Old Testament. Where the knife was bared, where the blood flowed, where could be

131

smelled the odor of smoking flesh, there occurred the great encounter.

Raise the stone and thou shalt find me,
Cleave the wood and there am I.
—Henry Van Dyke

In the New Testament it is the same. God still meets man at the point of sacrifice. But now there is a difference. It is at the point of his own sacrifice that he meets us, and it is at the point of that sacrifice that we must meet him with our sacrifice.

347. THE RICHES OF GOD

The Bible has something to say about the material riches of God; but it has much more to say about his spiritual wealth.

It speaks of:
1. The riches of his goodness. "Despisest thou the riches of his goodness?" Rom. 2:4
2. The riches of his grace. "In whom we have redemption through his blood, the forgiveness of sins, according to the riches of his grace." Eph. 1:7
3. The riches of his glory. "That he would grant you, according to the riches of his glory, to be strengthened with might by his Spirit in the inner man." Eph. 3:16

348. THE FREEDOM OF A CHRISTIAN MAN

Romans 5–8

According to Anders Nygren, the freedom of the Christian man,

132

as set forth in this spiritual Magna Carta, the Epistle to the Romans, is fourfold:
1. It is freedom from wrath.
Rom. 5
2. It is freedom from sin.
Rom. 6
3. It is freedom from law.
Rom. 7
4. It is freedom from death.
Rom. 8

349. THE LOVE OF GOD

"God commendeth his love toward us, in that, while we were yet sinners, Christ died for us."
Rom. 5:8

1. It is of the nature of love, as we know it, to desire the highest good of the one who is loved.
2. It is the nature of love, as we know it, to be willing to give itself to the one who is loved in order to impart the highest good.
3. It is the nature of love, as we know it, to want to possess its object.

—John A. Redhead, Jr.,
Getting to Know God

350. WHAT THE DEATH OF CHRIST WAS

"God commendeth his love toward us, in that, while we were yet sinners, Christ died for us."
Rom. 5:8

1. It was not a heroic martyrdom.
Like the death of Socrates.
2. It was not a bewildering tragedy.

Like the assassination of Lincoln or Kennedy.
3. It was a divine act.
"God commendeth his love . . . Christ died."

—John Wood,
The Preacher's Workshop

351. WHAT ADOPTION MEANS

"*Ye have received the Spirit of adoption.*" Rom. 8:15

By receiving the Spirit of adoption, we get:
1. A new Father.
2. A new family.
3. A new fortune.
4. A new future.
   All old debts are cancelled; the old life is done away.

352. ADOPTION

"*Ye have received the Spirit of adoption.*" Rom. 8:15

One of the most touching scenes I have ever witnessed was enacted in the waiting room of a hospital for unmarried mothers in the east end of London. A married lady attached to the church I then served was unable to have any children of her own and had decided to adopt a little boy. In the hospital an illegitimate baby had been born, and the mother, deeply attached to the child though she was, felt that she was unable to rear him. So an adoption was arranged. I was asked to be present when the real mother handed over her baby to the foster-mother. I shall never forget the poignancy of that moment. "Kiss him for the last time,"

said the probation officer, steeled by frequent experience to the pathos of the occasion. "Kiss him for the last time and put him into the arms of his new mother." There, confronting one another, stood the two women. On the face of the one were signs of the terrific struggle through which she was passing, while the face of the other was lit up with love and delighted anticipation. Quite unconscious of what was taking place, the sleeping baby changed hands; and by that transaction his whole life was affected.

The incident set me thinking about the radical revolution wrought in human lives by the spiritual experience of adoption. It was the contrast between them which particularly impressed me.
1. There is the contrast between the unconscious and the conscious.
   In natural adoption the baby is unconscious of what is taking place: in spiritual adoption the subject is fully conscious of the wonder of the new relationship. "Whereby we cry, Abba, Father."
   Rom. 8:15
2. There is the contrast between the involuntary and the voluntary.
   From the fact that the baby is unconscious, it follows that, even if it were capable of exercising the power of choice, it could have no say in the matter. It is adopted whether or not it wants to be.
   In a town in the south of Scotland live a Presbyterian

133

minister and his wife who were married some ten years ago. On returning from their honeymoon they found on the doorstep of the manse a basket containing a little colored boy. Around the baby's neck was a ribbon to which was attached a note begging them to adopt him and bring him up. They did. A most attractive little fellow he was. They called him "Georgie," and for a number of years now he has been a general favorite with that minister's congregation. A friend of mine who is a member of the church, told me that once, when the minister ascended the pulpit, the tiny colored lad, with shining face, cried out: "That's my Daddy!" Not often has that congregation been moved as it was by the excited exclamation of that little adoptee. Yet, in the first instance, the little fellow had no chance to choose whether or not he would belong to the new family. He was left on the doorstep, and that was that.

With spiritual adoption it is otherwise. Before it can take place, there must be a definite decision for Christ. "As many as received him, to them gave he power to become the sons of God, even to them that believe on his name."   John 1:12

3. There is the contrast between the legal and the vital. Natural adoption does not change the nature of the person to whom it happens: it simply alters his status. When Pharaoh's daughter adopted Moses, she did not make him an Egyptian: he was a Hebrew still. But when God adopts us into his family he imparts to us new life. In the relevant passage of Matthew Henry's *Commentary* there is this note: "Men may give a charter of adoption; but it is God's prerogative, when he adopts, to give a Spirit of adoption—the nature of children."

353. A WORLD IN PAIN

"For we know that the whole creation groaneth and travaileth in pain together until now."
                Rom. 8:22

It is characteristic of Paul that when he refers, as he does here, to the pain of the world, he speaks of it not as death throes but as birth pangs.

What is the purpose of pain?

While one is actually bearing it, there often appears to be no purpose in it whatever, and all one then longs for is its alleviation or removal. Afterwards, however, when one is detached enough from it to be philosophical about it, one perceives in the main four functions which it fulfills:

1. It is a signal indicating that something is wrong.
2. It is a preventive, intended to deter its victim from a repetition of the course of action which produced it.

3. It is a refiner of character in those who rightly respond to it.
4. It is the indispensable precondition of birth and growth.

354. CASE DISMISSED

"Who shall lay anything to the charge of God's elect?"
Rom. 8:33
"Who is he that condemneth?"
Rom. 8:34
"Who shall separate us from the love of Christ?" Rom. 8:35

1. There is no charge.
   "Who shall lay anything to the charge of God's elect?"
2. There is no judge.
   "Who is he that condemneth?"
3. There is no jailer.
   "Who shall separate us from the love of Christ?"

—Ian Macpherson,
None Other Name

355. HOW TO BE SAVED

(An Evangelistic Sermon)

"If thou shalt confess with thy mouth the Lord Jesus, and shalt believe in thine heart that God hath raised him from the dead, thou shalt be saved." Rom 10:9

Nobody is ever bothered in the least about being saved until he realizes that he is in danger. Are we in danger? We are because of temptation, sin, and the consequences of sin.

How, then, can we be saved? Let the text explain.
1. What the mouth must say.

"If thou shalt confess with thy mouth."
Confess what?
a) Jesus as living.
b) Jesus as Lord.
2. What the heart must do.
"And believe in thine heart"
—not just believe *in* Jesus, but believe *on* him.
3. What the life will show.
"Thou shalt be saved."

356. THREE SORTS OF FAITH

"Faith cometh by hearing."
Rom. 10:17

There are three sorts of faith:
1. The faith of assent.
   When the mind is convinced of the truth.
2. The faith of acceptance.
   When the will acts in accordance with the truth.
3. The faith of assurance.
   When the heart warms with the feeling of the truth.

—John Flavel (adapted)

357. LIFE IN THE BODY OF CHRIST

Rom. 12

1. The worship we are to offer.
   Rom. 12:1, 2
2. The service we are to render.
   Rom. 12:3-8
3. The love we are to display.
   a) to other Christians.
   Rom. 12:9-13
   b) to unbelievers.
   Rom. 12:14-21

—John Wood,
The Preacher's Workshop

135

358. GOD IS A GOOD PAYER

"I will repay, saith the Lord."
Rom. 12:19

Some people are known to tradesmen as "bad payers." They have a constitutional reluctance to discharge their debts. Such persons, oddly enough, are quite often very good buyers. Usually, they are more than ready to run up large accounts. So long as anyone is prepared to give them credit, they are only too eager to avail themselves of it. But when it comes to *paying* —ah, that is another matter! They are bad payers.

God is not like that. He never fails to meet his creditors. He is never slow in settling his accounts. He is no man's debtor. "I will repay, saith the Lord."

Notice three directions in which that is true.

1. He pays most liberally for things lent to him.
   If he borrows anything, he amply compensates the lender for the loan. As one has written:

God never leaves us in His debt. He takes care to pay for His entertainment, royally and divinely. He uses Peter's fishing-smack, and gives it back heavily submerged by the weight of the fish which He had driven into the nets. He sits down with His friends to a country marriage-feast, and pays for their simple fare by jars brimming with water turned to wine. He uses the five barley loaves, and two small fishes; but He fills the lad with an ample meal. He sends His prophet to lodge with a widow, and provides meal and oil for him and her for many days.

2. He pays in punishment for sins committed.
3. He paid the price of our redemption.
4. He pays in recompense for services rendered.

359. THREE WAYS OF LIVING

"Be not overcome of evil, but overcome evil with good."
Rom. 12:21

1. Some people do evil for good.
   That is human depravity.
2. Some people do good for good.
   That is civil retribution.
3. Some people do good for evil.
   That is Christian perfection.

—Unknown

360. REVEILLE

"The night is far spent, the day is at hand!"   Rom. 13:12

This is the call of the sentry on duty on the tented field. He wakes first, and it his duty to arouse the host of soldiers who lie sleeping around him in the camp.

Let us watch the scene as it changes from dark to light, from stillness to commotion.

1. There is a gleam in the sky.
2. There is a stir in the camp.
3. There is an army in the field.

—David Burns,
Sayings in Symbol

361. THE WEB OF LIFE

"For none of us liveth to himself."   Rom. 14:7

1. No man is an isolated unit.
2. Others have their share of right in what a man is and has.
3. Every man is in some measure indebted to others.
4. Every man's life should be controlled by the fact of relation.

—R. J. Wardell, *A Manual of Sermon Construction*

362. THREE TYPES OF MINISTERS

(An Ordination Sermon)

"I am sure that, when I come unto you, I shall come in the fulness of the blessing of the gospel of Christ." Rom. 15:29

1. There are those who say: "Here I am: let me do all I can for you."
   They are the bondslaves of their congregations.
2. There are those who say: "Here I am: do all you can for me."
   They are the private chaplains of their congregations.
3. There are those who say: "Here is Jesus Christ: let us together do all we can for him."
   They are the ambassadors of God to their congregations.

—John Snape

I CORINTHIANS

363. THE PROBLEMS OF A PRIMITIVE CHURCH

(An Outline of I Corinthians)

We are apt to think that the primitive church had no problems. On that point Paul's first epistle to the Corinthians puts us right. It is an extremely practical letter, dealing with difficulties which had arisen in the local Christian community.

What were those problems?

1. The problem of partiality. "Every one of you saith, I am of Paul; and I of Apollos; and I of Cephas; and I of Christ." I Cor. 1:12
2. The problem of immorality. "It is reported commonly that there is fornication among you." I Cor. 5:1
3. The problem of legality. "Dare any of you, having a matter against another, go to law before the unjust, and not before the saints?" I Cor. 6:1
4. The problem of morality. "Now as touching things offered unto idols, we know that we have all knowledge." I Cor. 8:1
5. The problem of spirituality. "Now concerning spiritual gifts, brethren, I would not have you ignorant." I Cor. 12:1
6. The problem of immortality. "Now if Christ be preached that he rose from the dead, how say some among you that there is no resurrection of the dead?" I Cor. 15:12

137

7. The problem of liberality. "Now concerning the collection for the saints, as I have given order to the churches of Galatia, even so do ye."

I Cor. 16:1

364. COMMON USES OF THE CROSS SYMBOL

"The word of the cross."

I Cor. 1:18 RSV

Not only is the cross a symbol in religion. It is a sign we often use in everyday life. Consider some of these secular usages of the cross and note their spiritual analogies.

We employ the cross as:

1. A sign of correction.
   We "cross" out what is wrong.
   A little girl returned radiant from school one day. "What makes you so happy?" asked her mother. "It's because I now know that the teacher loves me," explained the child. "And how do you know that?" queried her parent. "Because she put a kiss opposite every sum I did today!" the little one announced, triumphantly.
2. A token of affection.
   We use the cross for the kiss. Taken to church for the first time, a tiny boy was fascinated by the stained-glass window above the altar, on which was emblazoned a crimson cross. Asked later what he liked best in the service, he replied: "God's kiss on the window!"

3. A mark of identification.
   X, we say, marks the spot. Wherever a fatal accident occurs on the roads of Switzerland or Western Australia, a white cross is painted and kept perpetually bright as a constant reminder and warning to motorists.
4. A symbol in mathematics.
   It stands for addition and multiplication.
   On a wall of the parish church at Tenby, Pembrokeshire, there is a memorial plaque to a man named Robert Recorde, who was born in that town (circa 1510) and who invented the mathematical sign of equivalence. I have never seen a memorial to the man who first thought of using the cross as a symbol of addition and multiplication. He deserved one. It was certainly an inspired idea, for "the cross is God's plus sign for our minus lives."
5. A sign of decision.
   In the polling booth we put X on the ballot card opposite the name of the candidate for whom we wish to vote in a political election.
   When we take up his cross, we vote for Jesus Christ.

365. THE CROSS AS A SIGNPOST

"The preaching of the cross."

I Cor. 1:18

There is a story, amusing yet affecting, about an old man who, when dying, said he had something on his mind which he wanted to confess to a minister. The minister was called to his bedside, and the old man told him how, long years before, when he was a boy, he had seen two men on a common fixing a signpost. After the men had gone, he had turned the signpost around and had made it point in the wrong direction. All his life, he confided, he had been haunted by the thought that he had thus sent so many travellers the wrong way.

It is indeed a despicable thing to take advantage of people's ignorance and set them on the false trail.

The cross never does that. It, too, is a signpost, and its direction is infallible.

Note that:

1. The cross of Christ is a signpost pointing us back to where we came from.
   It shows us, as does nothing else, the depths of depravity in the human heart.
2. The cross of Christ is a signpost pointing up to what we were meant to be.
3. The cross of Christ is a signpost pointing on to what we are going to be.

366. THE WEAKNESS OF GOD

"The weakness of God is stronger than men." I Cor. 1:25

"The weakness of God." What a curious phrase! How utterly contrary to our common conceptions of him! How completely contradictory of our thought of him as omnipotent! Weakness, it might well seem, is one thing which it is logically impossible to predicate of God!

Yet here stand the words of the great apostle—"the weakness of God." The conjunction of conceptions is striking and stimulative. Weakness—God! It leads us to reflect that in this regard there are really three sorts of persons.

1. There are those who are weak because they cannot be anything else.
   Nature has made them so. They are weak, it may be, physically, mentally, or morally.
2. There are those who are strong and not weak at all.
3. There are those who, although strong, deliberately choose to be weak.
   Of this sort of person God is the supreme example. His voluntary weakness is seen most conspicuously in his becoming a babe, fasting in the wilderness, and dying on the Cross.

367. THE CHRISTIAN'S BELONGINGS

"All things are yours."
I Cor. 3:21

1. All things belong to the Christian because none but his God has the power to bestow them.
2. All things belong to the Christian because none but he has the faculty fully to enjoy them.
3. All things belong to the Christian because from him no one can take them away.

139

John Newton, author of several of our best-known hymns, called once on a family that had recently lost everything in a fire. To the mother he said: "I give you joy, Madam." Surprised, and ready to take offense at his seeming flippancy and heartlessness, she retorted: "What! Joy that all my property is consumed?" "Oh, no," answered Newton, "but joy that you have so much property that cannot be touched by fire!"

368. PAULINE METAPHORS OF THE CHRISTIAN MINISTRY

"Though ye have ten thousand instructors in Christ, yet have ye not many fathers: for in Christ Jesus I have begotten you through the gospel." I Cor. 4:15
"The husbandman that laboreth must be first partaker of the fruits." II Tim. 2:6
"Thou therefore endure hardness, as a good soldier of Jesus Christ." II Tim. 2:3
"Now then we are ambassadors for Christ." II Cor. 5:20
"As a wise master builder, I have laid the foundation." I Cor. 3:10

The following five figures illustrate how Paul thought of himself as a Christian minister. He pictured himself in the relation of:

1. A father to his family.
2. A husbandman with his plants.
3. A soldier with his enemies.
4. An ambassador with his king.
5. A builder with his structure.

—J. Reginald Hill, *How to Illustrate Your Lessons*

369. LIVING TEMPLES

"Know ye not that your body is the temple of the Holy Ghost?" I Cor. 6:19

There can, indeed, be no house for God. Beyond him there can be nothing. God is, therefore, the sole temple of God.

Yet there is a sense in which, as Paul reminds us in the text, every Christian is a house in which God dwells.

1. Every true Christian is a house of worship.
   A temple is a place where God's presence is felt.
2. Every true Christian is a house of wisdom.
   In the ancient temple the scribes sat teaching.
3. Every true Christian is a house of witness.
   The very existence of a temple is a public reminder of the reality of God.
4. Every true Christian is a house of welcome.
   All were invited. Trumpets rang out a welcome. Loud voices from its pinnacles bade people come to the house of God.

—David Burns, *Sayings in Symbol*

370. SPIRITUAL OLYMPICS

"So run, that ye may obtain." I Cor. 9:24

Three conditions were imposed on all would-be competitors in the ancient games at Corinth. He who would qualify as an entrant must satisfy the examiners on all the following three points:

1. He must be a citizen of Corinth.
2. He must have a good reputation.
3. He must willingly offer himself.

Apply this spiritually.

—Unknown

371. CHRIST THE ROCK

"That Rock was Christ."
I Cor. 10:4

This is a brilliantly illuminative flash, a spark struck from the flinty mind of the apostle. "That Rock was Christ." It is a striking, if incidental, indication of how completely Paul's thoughts were occupied with his master. He finds Christ everywhere—even in a bare rock amid the desert sands.

Can the figure be sustained? How is Christ like a rock?

1. He is like a rock in his impregnable solidity.
2. He is like a rock in his unchanging durability.
3. He is like a rock, this rock, inasmuch as he was smitten. Matthew Henry quotes "the learned Bishop Patrick" as referring to "the smitten rock out of which one would rather expect fire than water."
"One of the soldiers with a spear pierced his side, and

forthwith came there out . . . water." John 19:34
4. He is like this rock forasmuch as, in the wilderness of this world, he is the sole source of life.

372. TEMPTATION

"There hath no temptation taken you but such as is common to man: but God is faithful, who will not suffer you to be tempted above that ye are able; but will with the temptation also make a way to escape, that ye may be able to bear it." I Cor. 10:13

We learn from this that:

1. Temptation is inevitable.
2. Temptation is necessary.
3. Temptation is revelatory of character.
4. Temptation is adjusted by God.
5. Temptation is bearable.

—J. Gregory Mantle,
God's Tomorrow

373. THE LORD'S TABLE

"The Lord's table."
I Cor. 10:21

I wonder when Jesus first possessed a table. Was it perhaps when, as an apprentice to his trade, he made one as a carpenter at Nazareth? Or was it later when, his foster-father Joseph having died, he himself became a householder and welcomed people round his hospitable board? I don't know. Certainly, the table around which the disciples sat in the Upper Room at the institution of the sacrament did not belong to Christ.

141

It was borrowed. Yet in a peculiar sense it was the table of the Lord. And everytime the fair linen cloth is spread and Christ's followers gather round the festal board, it is the Lord's table still. Observe that it is:

1. A table, not a tomb.
   At the Sacrament we assemble not merely to commemorate Christ, but to communicate with him. He is not a dead memory: He is a living presence.
2. A table, not an altar.
   Had Jesus wanted to take his disciples to an altar, he could have conducted them to the Temple. There was an altar there, dripping with blood and reeking with smoke. Instead he led them to a house and gathered with them round a table.
3. A table, not a desk.
   The desk, and the scholarship for which it stands, is indeed an important element in the Christian religion. The supreme experience of our faith, however, is not the intellectual correspondence of theology, but the spiritual communion of the sacramental table.

374. TOGETHER

"When ye come together . . . I hear that there be divisions among you." I Cor. 11:18
"When ye come together . . . tarry one for another." I Cor. 11:33
"When ye come together, every one of you hath a psalm, hath a doctrine, hath a tongue, hath a

revelation, hath an interpretation." I Cor. 14:26

That word "together" is one of the key words of the New Testament. The Greek term *homou* is from the same root as *homoios,* meaning "like." "Birds of a feather fly together," we say. Like draws to like.

This is true in every sphere. Every voluntary association is a living illustration of it.

It is peculiarly true of the Christian church.

"When ye come together"—what happens?

1. Differences become intolerable.
   "I hear that divisions exist among you."
   Togetherness in the physical sense makes mental and spiritual togetherness absolutely essential. Two ministers were visiting a mental hospital one day. Around them in the great institution were thousands of patients in various stages of insanity. "Wouldn't it be terrible if all these lunatics were to unite against us?" asked one of the visitors of the other. "Don't worry," came the reply, "lunatics never unite!"
2. Communion becomes possible.
   "When ye come together to eat."
3. Ministry becomes communal.
   "When ye come together, every one of you hath a psalm," and so forth.

375. THE BROKEN BODY

"This is my body, which is broken for you." I Cor. 11:24

1. This is my body.
   That speaks of the Incarnation.
2. Broken.
   That speaks of the Crucifixion.
3. For you.
   That speaks of the need for appropriation.

376. WHY DID JESUS WANT TO BE REMEMBERED?

(A Communion Sermon)

"This do in remembrance of me." I Cor. 11:24

Why do you think Jesus said that? Was he afraid that he would be forgotten? Surely not! Nobody could ever forget Jesus. Was he, then, apprehensive lest he would not rise from the dead and so disappear altogether from the recollection of his disciples? Not so. "I have power to lay down my life," He said, "and I have power to take it again." John 10:18 He who spoke thus was not in fear of extinction. No! Those were not the reasons why our Lord desired to be remembered in the breaking of the bread and the pouring of the wine. Rather was it that our hearts might be kept soft and tender by the constantly renewed sacrament of love.

In this holy ordinance we have:

1. Commemoration of an absent Lord.
   "Till he come."
   I Cor. 11:26

Evidently, then, he is not here in physical presence.
2. Communication with a present Lord.
   "Where two or three are gathered together in my name, there am I in the midst of them."
   Matt. 18:20
3. Contemplation of a coming Lord.
   "Ye do show the Lord's death till he come."
   I Cor. 11:26

377. CHRIST'S BODY AND OURS

"This is my body." I Cor. 11:24b.
"Your body is the temple of the Holy Ghost." I Cor. 6:19
"Present your bodies a living sacrifice." Rom. 12:1

Note that:

1. The sinner says: "Your body is mine."
   Slavery, prostitution, sweated labor, etc.
2. The moralist says: "My body is my own."
3. Christ says: "My body is yours."
4. The Christian says: "My body belongs to Christ."
   To be indwelt by him and to work for him.

378. THE TRUE RELIGION

"Though I speak with the tongues of men and of angels, and have not charity, I am become as sounding brass, or a tinkling cymbal. And though I have the gift of prophecy, and understand all mysteries, and all knowledge; and though I have

143

faith, so that I could remove mountains, and have not charity, I am nothing. And though I bestow all my goods to feed the poor, and though I give my body to be burned, and have not charity, it profiteth me nothing."

I Cor. 13:1-3

Here we have presented to us:

1. Religion as ecstatic emotionalism.
   "Though I speak with the tongues of men and of angels."
2. Religion as intellectualism, speculation.
   "Though I have the gift of prophecy, and understand all mysteries, and all knowledge."
3. Religion as working energy.
   "Though I have all faith, so that I could remove mountains."
4. Religion as humanitarianism.
   "Though I bestow all my goods to feed the poor."
5. Religion as asceticism.
   "Though I give my body to be burned."
6. Religion as perfect love.
   "Charity."

—James S. Stewart,
A Man In Christ

379. THE SUPERIORITY OF THOSE WHO LOVE

"Though I speak with the tongues of men and of angels, and have not charity, I am become as sounding brass, or a tinkling cymbal. And though I have the gift of prophecy, and understand all mysteries, and all knowledge; and though I have all faith, so that I

could remove mountains, and have not charity, I am nothing. And though I bestow all my goods to feed the poor, and though I give my body to be burned, and have not charity, it profiteth me nothing."

I Cor. 13:1-3

Of those who love, this chapter says that:

1. They are superior to those who merely say.
   "Though I speak."
2. They are superior to those who merely know.
   "Though I understand all mysteries."
3. They are superior to those who merely do.
   "Though I have all faith, so that I could remove mountains."
4. They are superior to those who merely give.
   "Though I bestow all my goods to feed the poor, and though I give my body to be burned."

Footnote: Of course, those who love will speak, know, do, and give more and better than all.

380. WHY DID JESUS DIE?

To that interrogation the New Testament supplies three direct answers:

It says that Christ died:

1. To satisfy divine law.
   "Christ died for our sins."
   I Cor. 15:3
2. To exemplify divine love.
   "Christ died for us."
   Rom. 5:8
3. To ratify divine Lordship.
   Rom. 14:9

381. DIMINISHING SELF-ESTIMATE

It is strange to find Paul professedly thinking less of himself in proportion as, by reason of his maturing mind and massing achievements, he was surely entitled to think more of himself.

Yet such was the case.

He describes himself successively as:

1. The least of the apostles.
   I Cor. 15:9
2. Less than the least of all saints. Eph. 3:8
3. The chief of sinners.
   I Tim. 1:15

Footnote: "If Paul was less than the least of all saints, what size are you?"—Spurgeon

382. SOMETHING TO SHOUT ABOUT

"Now is Christ risen from the dead." I Cor. 15:20

In a graceful tribute to her father, the daughter of the late W. E. Sangster depicts a poignant and deeply moving scene. For the last two years of his life the great preacher was afflicted with a distressing disease—disseminated sclerosis—which gradually deprived him of the power of speech and of the use of his limbs. Toward the end, his condition rapidly worsened and all he could do was communicate with his loved ones by means of a writing pad. As the anniversary of Christ's resurrection came round in 1960, he grew strangely excited, as he always did, at the prospect of celebrating the glorious occasion; and when the actual day dawned he reached for his pad and wrote this: "Easter Day!—the day when one wants to shout. What a pity not to be able to shout! But— what a tragedy it would be not to *want* to shout!"

The resurrection of Jesus Christ is certainly something to shout about. Why?

1. Because it means that the tyranny of the tomb is broken. "Thanks be to God, which giveth us the victory through our Lord Jesus Christ."
   I Cor. 15:57
2. Because it means the possibility of a moral resurrection for ourselves. "That I may know him, and the power of his resurrection." Phil. 3:10
3. Because it means that power is available for the revitalization of the church. "That ye may know . . . what is the exceeding greatness of his power to us-ward who believe, according to the working of his mighty power, which he wrought in Christ, when he raised him from the dead." Eph. 1:18-20
4. Because it means the prospect of personal survival for us all. "Christ [is] . . . become the firstfruits of them that slept."
   I Cor. 15:20

383. WHERE, GRAVE, THY VICTORY?

"O grave, where is thy victory?" I Cor. 15:55

That was a bold taunt to fling in the face of a triumphant tomb.

145

"Where is thy victory?" You might as well have asked that of Alexander the Great when, at the height of his power, he was lord of the whole earth. You might as well have asked it of Julius Caesar when his conquests were coterminous with the habitable world. You might have asked it of Napoleon when he bade fair to be master of mankind.

"Where is thy victory?" The grave might have answered: "Everywhere!"

It is, indeed, a daring taunt; and yet I bid you notice that:

1. Memory flings it in the face of the grave.
   It is true that "the faded photograph is not the living face." Yet memory has a photograph of the beloved dead which will not fade while life lasts.
2. Love flings it in the face of the grave.
   Among the most moving lines ever written are these by Emily Brontë, penned of a dead lover:

Cold in the earth
—and the deep snow piled above thee

Far, far removed,
    cold in the dreary grave!
Have I forgot,
    my only Love, to love thee,
Sever'd at last
    by Time's all-severing wave?

The chill of the tomb pierced her to the bone, and yet her love triumphed over the tomb.
3. Influence flings it in the face of the grave.
   Many dead men have more power than most who are alive today. Their influence lives on. They "rule us from their urns." They, like "Abel . . . being dead yet speak." Heb. 11:4
4. Christ flings it in the face of the grave.
   "He it was who turned the death-day of a child into a birth-day, whom the funeral could not pass and at whose word the tomb gave up its prey."
5. The Christian may, by faith in Jesus, likewise fling that taunt in the face of the grave.
   "Where is thy victory, O grave?"
   "God giveth us the victory."

II CORINTHIANS

384. DOORS THAT ARE NEVER LOCKED

"A door was opened unto me."
II Cor. 2:12

Let us consider:

1. The door of duty.
2. The door of suffering.
3. The door of prayer.

—J. Price Williams, *All Clear*

385. LIVING VICTORIOUSLY

"Thanks be to God who leads us, wherever we are, on his own triumphant way."

II Cor. 2:14 Phillips

Edwin Markham, the American poet, was expected to arrive by train at a certain town, and a local minister went to the station to meet him. As the venerable man of letters stepped down from the car, the minister greeted him. "Well, Dr. Markham, how are you?" The aged saint and philosopher-poet with flowing hair and flashing eyes replied with a shout: "I am living victoriously!"

That is how every Christian should be living.

What does it imply?

1. It means the conquest of self.
2. It means the defeat of doubt.
3. It means the mastery of circumstance.

All this is possible to us through Christ, and through Christ alone.

386. OPEN LETTERS

"You are an open letter."

II Cor. 3:3 Phillips

It comes to us as something of a surprise to reflect that the New Testament is, very largely, a bundle of letters. There are in all twenty-nine letters in the Christian scriptures. Most of them we call epistles. They are from the pens of Paul, Peter, James, John, and Jude, and there are a score of them. But other parts of the New Testament are letters too. The Gospel of Luke is a letter. The book of Acts is a letter. And in the book of Revelation there are recorded no fewer than seven letters addressed by the risen Christ to the churches of Asia Minor.

These are not, however, the only letters connected with the Christian religion. In our text Paul tells us that every Christian is a letter, and the number of such letters is impossible to assess.

When you come to think of it, is there not something singularly fitting and suggestive in the figure? For consider:

1. A letter is a very personal thing.

It is usually directed by a person to a person. Unlike a literary composition, it is not intended for publication, but is generally "a word in the ear" sent to some particular individual.

"Do you do any literary work?" asked a neighbor of a mother. "Yes," she replied. "I am writing two books." "What are their titles?" "John and Mary," she answered. "My business is to write upon the minds and hearts of my children the lessons that they shall never forget."

—Moody Monthly

2. A letter is a very urgent thing.

It is foolish to write a letter and then forget to post it. As soon as it is penned, it is posted. And the swift transport and delivery of our mail is one of the amenities of the modern world which we tend to take for granted. Everybody assumes that letters are urgent.

147

3. A letter presupposes separation and seeks to annihilate it.
A letter is a paper bridge. It unites those whom distance divides. And we, as letters of Christ, are meant to be a bridge between the church and the world.
4. A letter calls for a reply. Napoleon said that if you put off answering letters for a fortnight you generally found that they had answered themselves. But that is a practice alike discourteous and impolitic. R.S.V.P.

387. A THREEFOLD CONTRAST

"Though our outward man perish, yet the inward man is renewed day by day. For our light affliction, which is but for a moment, worketh for us a far more exceeding and eternal weight of glory."
II Cor. 4:16-18

Observe here a threefold contrast:

1. There is the contrast between the passing and the permanent.
"But for a moment . . . eternal."
2. There is the contrast between the exterior and the interior.
"Our outward man . . . the inward man."
3. There is the contrast between the paltry and the ponderable.
"Our light affliction . . . weight of glory."

148

388. IN PRAISE OF AMBITION

"Wherefore we are ambitious . . . to be well-pleasing unto him."
II Cor. 5:9
"But we exhort you, brethren, that ye increase more and more; and that ye be ambitious to be quiet."
I Thess. 4:10, 11
"Be ambitious to show thyself approved unto God."
II Tim. 2:15

Consider:

1. Ambition in character.
2. Ambition in duty.
3. Ambition in service.

—W. L. Watkinson, *Moral Paradoxes of St. Paul*

389. THE UNIVERSALITY OF THE DEATH OF CHRIST

"Christ died for all."
II Cor. 5:15

You may remember how in "The Elephant's Child" Rudyard Kipling writes:

I keep six honest serving-men
(They taught me all I knew);
Their names are What and Why and When
And How and Where and Who.

Let us ask three of these serving-men to interrogate the text:

1. What does the word "died" mean?
More than mere physical dissolution.
2. How could he die for all?
Because of what he was.
3. Why did he die for all?

Because of the love of God
and the worth of man.

—R. J. Wardell, *A Manual of
Sermon Construction*

390. THE NEW MAN

"*Wherefore if any man be in
Christ, he is a new creature.*"
II Cor. 5:17

Note that:

1. He possesses a new life.
2. He belongs to a new land.
3. He obeys a new law.
4. He engages in a new labor.

—Unknown

391. CHRIST AS THE MASTER OF TIME

"*Now is the accepted time.*"
II Cor. 6:2

All our life we have been the slave
of time.
Christ is the Lord of time.
Here are three simple truths about
time:

1. The past is not dead.
2. The future is not ours.
3. Now is the acceptable time.

—W. E. Sangster,
Sangster's Special-Day Sermons

392. THE ABUNDANT LIFE

A true Christian is simply bound
to abound.

His is:

1. Abundance of faith.
   "Abound . . . in faith."
   II Cor. 8:7
2. Abundance of hope.
   "Abound in hope."
   Rom. 15:13

3. Abundance of love.
   "Abound in love."
   Phil. 1:9
4. Abundance of good works.
   "Abound to every good
   work." II Cor. 9:8

393. THE RICHES OF CHRIST

"*Ye know the grace of our Lord
Jesus Christ, that, though he was
rich, yet for your sakes he became
poor, that ye through his poverty
might be rich.*" II Cor. 8:9

1. How rich he was!
2. How poor he became!
3. How wealthy he made us!

—Andrew W. Blackwood,
Doctrinal Preaching for Today

394. A MEDITATION FOR CHRISTMAS

"*For ye know the grace of our
Lord Jesus Christ, that, though he
was rich, yet for your sakes he became poor, that ye through his
poverty might be rich.*"
II Cor. 8:9

1. There are his riches to consider.
   "He was rich."
2. There is his poverty to consider.
   "He became poor."
3. There are our riches to consider.
   "That we might be rich."
   Many of the rich of this
   world are rich because of our
   poverty; Christ has made us
   rich by his poverty. By his
   poverty, note: not by his
   riches.

—John A. Duke,
The Untroubled Heart

149

395. WHAT CAN WE GIVE GOD?

"Thanks be unto God for his un-speakable gift." II Cor. 9:15

There are three kinds of gifts:

1. The present-with-a-purpose, the bribe. Given with a view to obtaining something for the donor.
2. The duty gift. Given from a sense of obligation.
3. The love gift. Given for the sake of affection.

—David H. C. Read,
Sons of Anak

396. THE SIMPLICITY OF CHRIST

"The simplicity that is in Christ." II Cor. 11:3

Consider:

1. The simplicity in the life of Jesus Christ.
   a) in its main outward features.
   b) inwardly.
2. The simplicity of the doctrine of Jesus Christ.
   a) His doctrine of God—"Our Father."
   b) His doctrine of salvation —"For God so loved the world," and so forth.
3. The simplicity of Christ's rule of duty.
   "Follow me."
   "Thou shalt love the Lord thy God," etc.

—James Dinwoodie,
Illustrated Sermon Outlines

397. PAUL'S THORN

"There was given to me a thorn in the flesh, the messenger of Satan to buffet me, lest I should be exalted above measure."
II Cor. 12:7

It has been well said that Paul's thorn in the flesh has been a thorn to many. There have been all sorts of speculations as to what it really was—epilepsy, neurasthenia, ophthalmia, and what not. Ophthalmia is the most probable. In the Old Testament the same word for thorn in the flesh is translated "prick in the eyes." Paul, we recall, was blinded by the heavenly vision, and of the Galatians he said that they would have plucked out their very eyes and given them to him. Besides, Paul did not write his epistles himself, but merely signed his name at the end "in large characters."

Yes, it may have been ophthalmia. Whatever it was, we gather that it was permitted to remain for a purpose.

It was:

1. Something to keep him humble.
2. Something to make him feel his weakness.
3. Something to send him repeatedly to Christ.

—John Mitchell, *Shot and Shell for the Preacher's Gun*
(adapted)

398. THE DISCIPLINE OF DISAPPOINTMENT

"Lest I should be exalted above measure through the abundance of the revelations, there was given

to me a thorn in the flesh . . . for when I am weak, then am I strong." II Cor. 12:7, 10

There are three simple words that sum up, it seems to me, the teaching of this passage:
1. Frustration.
   "There was given to me a thorn."
2. Revelation.
   "He said unto me."
3. Transformation.
   "When I am weak, then am I strong."

—George B. Duncan, Wanting the Impossible

399. THE TRINITY

"The grace of the Lord Jesus Christ, and the love of God, and the communion of the Holy Ghost, be with you all. Amen."
II Cor. 13:14
1. God transcendent.
   The Father.
2. God evident.
   The Lord Jesus Christ.
3. God immanent.
   The Holy Spirit.

400. THE TRINITY

"The grace of the Lord Jesus Christ, and the love of God, and the communion of the Holy Ghost, be with you all."
II Cor. 13:14
1. God the Father is the Lover.
2. God the Son is the Beloved.
3. God the Holy Spirit is the Love.

—Augustine of Hippo

GALATIANS

401. THE GOSPEL IS OF GOD

"I certify you, brethren, that the gospel which was preached of me is not after man. For I neither received it of man, neither was I taught it, but by the revelation of Jesus Christ." Gal. 1:11, 12
1. The gospel was not originated by man.
   "Not after man."
2. The gospel is not communicated by man.
   "Neither received it of man."
   Man may convey the letter: only God can convey the Spirit.
3. The gospel is not enunciated by man.
   "Neither was I taught it."
   It is a direct divine revelation to the believing soul.

402. A FAMOUS FIFTEEN DAYS

"I went up to Jerusalem to see Peter, and abode with him fifteen days." Gal. 1:18
A modern translator of the New Testament has said that Paul spent a fortnight's holiday with Peter at Jerusalem. If Paul did, it was a working holiday; one of the

151

most fruitful fortnights in human history.

1. Paul went to see Peter for firsthand information.

   The translation indicates that he went to see Peter, but the original word has a far greater amount of suggestion. Literally, it can be translated: "I went up to Jerusalem to *history* Peter."

2. Paul went to see Peter to impart revelation.

   He had been in Arabia, and there God had given him a deeper insight into his purpose for the church than had been vouchsafed to Peter himself.

3. Paul went to see Peter to secure cooperation.

   Although in his pioneering work Paul had to plow a lone furrow, he did not want to become an unconnected indidividualist. He wished to act in concert with the whole church of God.

—W. L. Stephen,
A Great Nation (adapted)

403. THE KIND OF LIFE PAUL LIVED

"The life which I now live in the flesh I live by the faith of the Son of God, who loved me and gave himself for me."   Gal. 2:20

What kind of life did the apostle live in the flesh by faith in the Son of God? Think of his sufferings, his missionary strategy, his final sacrifice. See the life of the apostle roll out as a panorama before you. You cannot but con-

152

clude that his life was one in which:

1. Nothing was too high to be attempted.
2. Nothing was too hard to be endured.
3. Nothing was too good to be hoped for.
4. Nothing was too precious to be given away.

—E. D. Jarvis,
If Any Man Minister

404. THREE CONTRASTS

"I have been crucified with Christ: nevertheless I live; yet not I, but Christ liveth in me." I, but Christ liveth in me."
Gal. 2:20

We have in this verse three contrasts presented to us:

1. The contrast between the past and the present.
   "The life which I now live."
2. The contrast between love and law.
   "The Son of God loved me" —previously Paul had lived under law.
3. The contrast between Christ and self.
   "Not I, but Christ."

—John Wood,
The Preacher's Workshop

405. EVERY BARRIER DOWN

"There is neither Jew nor Greek, there is neither bond nor free, there is neither male nor female: for ye all are one in Christ Jesus."
Gal. 3:28
"There is neither Greek nor Jew, circumcision nor uncircumcision,

*Barbarian, Scythian, bond nor free:
but Christ is all, and in all.*
Col. 3:11

In these texts we see Christianity transcending all the distinctions that divide mankind.

We see it stepping over barriers raised by:

1. Religious tradition.
   Neither Jew nor Gentile.
2. Ancient culture.
   Neither Greek nor Scythian.
3. Social and economic conditions.
   Neither bond nor free.
4. The sexes.
   Neither male nor female.

—Lumsden Barkway,
The Creed and Its Credentials

406. WHY BE GOOD?

*"The fruit of the Spirit is . . .
goodness."*   Gal. 5:22

Why should we be good?

Three answers may be offered to that question:

1. Because we're told to be.
   This is the authoritarian view.
   Various authorities:
   a) parental.
   b) scholastic.
   c) ecclesiastical.
   d) civil.
   e) national.
2. Because it pays us to be.
   This is the prudential view.
   Morality does pay high dividends:
   a) in physical health.
   b) in mental vigor.
   c) in social power.

   d) in psychological integration.
3. Because Christ impels and enables us to be.
   This is the evangelical view.
   How does Christ empower us to be good?
   a) by his example.
   b) by his teaching.
   c) by his indwelling.

407. THE MORAL HARVEST

"Be not deceived; God is not mocked: for whatsoever a man soweth, that shall he also reap."
Gal. 6:7

Years ago in Aberdeen a young man attended an evangelistic service being conducted in a tent. It was a Saturday evening and the large marquee was packed to capacity. At the close of his address the preacher issued an appeal. The young man felt that he ought to respond, but was reluctant to do so. At last the pressure put upon him became so great that he dashed out of the tent and threaded his way through the thronged streets of the town in the hope of escaping from the challenge of the gospel. Presently, he found himself approaching the entrance to a theater in which, as posters displayed on the billboards outside intimated, a play entitled "Major Barbara" by George Bernard Shaw was being performed. "Here," thought the young man, "I shall be safe from the strivings of the Holy Spirit." At the box office he paid for a seat in the gallery and made his way there as quickly as he could. As he sat down and looked at the brilliantly lit stage, he

153

suddenly realized that the play was about the Salvation Army. A half-circle of actresses, dressed in Salvationist uniforms, were pretending to conduct an open-air service. One of them stepped briskly to the front of the stage, and in a voice that resounded through the huge auditorium, exclaimed: "Be not deceived; God is not mocked: whatsoever a man soweth, that shall he also reap." "My God," cried the young man, "have you followed me even to a theater?" Rising up at once, he made his way back to the tent. The evangelist was just about to close his appeal. Among those who responded to it was the young man of our story.

The text issues its solemn warning to us too.

Consider:

1. The sowing.
   "Whatsoever a man soweth."
2. The growing.
   "Be not deceived." The issue of things does not immediately appear. It may look for a while as though wild oats yield no harvest, but an inevitable process of growth is taking place.
3. The mowing.
   "That shall he also reap."
   A friend, visiting Horatio Bottomley, the notorious swindler, in prison, found him sewing mailbags. "Hello, Bottomley," said the visitor. "Sewing?" "No," replied Bottomley, laconically, "reaping!"

154

408. THE INEVITABLE HARVEST

"Be not deceived; God is not mocked: for whatsoever a man soweth, that shall he also reap."
Gal. 6:7

We see here:

1. The issue of a warning.
   "Be not deceived."
2. The statement of a fact.
   "God is not mocked."
3. The operation of a law.
   "Whatsoever a man soweth, that shall he also reap."

409. THE SOUL AND THE CROSS

"But God forbid that I should glory, save in the cross of our Lord Jesus Christ, by whom the world is crucified unto me, and I unto the world."   Gal. 6:14

1. The soul at the cross.
   That is salvation.
2. The soul on the cross.
   That is sanctification.
3. The soul under the cross.
   That is submission, service.

410. THE CROSS AND THE SOUL

"God forbid that I should glory, save in the cross of our Lord Jesus Christ, by whom the world is crucified unto me, and I unto the world."   Gal. 6:14

Note that:

1. The cross evaluates the soul.
2. The cross emancipates the soul.
3. The cross elevates the soul.

411. WHAT PAUL TOOK PRIDE IN

"God forbid that I should glory, save in the cross of our Lord Jesus Christ, by whom the world is crucified unto me, and I unto the world. Gal. 6:14

Consider:

1. What Paul once gloried in:
   a) his pedigree.
   b) his birth.
   c) his education.
   d) his character.
   e) his rank as a Pharisee.
   f) his status as a Roman citizen.
2. What Paul might now have gloried in:
   a) his power as a preacher.
   b) his literary genius.
   c) his personal influence.
   d) his achievements as a Christian pioneer.
3. What Paul actually did glory in:
   the cross of Christ!

412. WHAT IS THE CROSS?

"But God forbid that I should glory, save in the cross of our Lord Jesus Christ." Gal. 6:14

What is the cross? That, you may say, is a silly and superfluous question. The cross? Why, it is just two bits of wood hammered together with a few nails! But is that all that there is in the cross? Far from it. Viewed with the eye of faith, the cross is the most marvelous thing in the world.

Let us see if we can capture some of its meaning in five crisp sentences. What is the cross? It is:

1. A key to unlock the meaning of life.
2. A lever to lift the burdens of life.
3. A balance to weigh the values of life.
4. A sword to fight the battles of life.
5. A ladder to raise the standard of life.

413. THE CROSS AS A KEY

"God forbid that I should glory, save in the cross of our Lord Jesus Christ." Gal. 6:14

In his book *Real Discipleship* T. Howard Crago tells of a conversation he once had with Le Fanu, Archbishop of Western Australia, in the course of which the latter related to him the following story. "When my little son was very young," said the Archbishop, "he wandered into my study one day and, picking up a small silver cross which was lying on the desk, asked: "Daddy, is this a key?' 'Yes, my son,' I replied, 'that *is* a key!' "

The cross as a key. That is our thought for today. Notice one or two of the ways in which this is true.

1. The cross is a key to the meaning of life.
2. The cross is a key to the prison of sin.
3. The cross is a key to the cell of uncongenial circumstance.
4. The cross is the key to the grave.

155

414. THE STIGMATA OF JESUS

"From henceforth let no man trouble me: for I bear in my body the marks of the Lord Jesus."
Gal. 6:17

Several thoughts are suggested by these words:

1. Ownership.
   "The marks"—"the owner's brand."
2. Sacrifice.
   "I bear in my body."
3. Liberty.
   "Let no man trouble me."
   It was the sign of his servitude to one master and of his freedom from all others.

—J. Gregory Mantle,
God's Tomorrow

EPHESIANS

415. THE BEGINNINGS OF THE CHRISTIAN LIFE

(As intimated in Paul's Epistle to the Ephesians.)
Let us note some of the experiences which the apostle describes:

1. Redemption from sin.
   "Jesus Christ . . . in whom we have redemption through his blood, the forgiveness of sins." Eph. 1:5, 7
2. Rescue from darkness.
   "Ye were sometime darkness, but now are ye light in the Lord." Eph. 5:8
3. Resurrection from death.
   "You hath he quickened, who were dead in trespasses and sins." Eph. 2:1
4. Release from captivity.
   "In time past ye walked according to the course of this world . . . but God . . . made us sit together in heavenly places in Christ Jesus." Eph. 2:2, 6
5. Return from exile.

"At that time ye were without Christ, being aliens . . . and strangers. . . . But now . . . ye . . . are made nigh." Eph. 2:12, 13
6. Reconciliation from enmity.
   "He is our peace, who hath made both one . . . having slain the enmity." Eph. 2:14, 16

—John Macbeath,
The Life of a Christian

416. SPIRITUAL PROMOTION

"Ye were without Christ . . . strangers." Eph. 2:12
"If any man serve me, let him follow me; and where I am, there shall also my servant be." John 12:26
"Henceforth I call you not servants; for the servant knoweth not what his lord doeth; but I have called you friends." John 15:15
"Go to my brethren." John 20:17

156

Note the three transitions:
1. From strangers to servants.
2. From servants to friends.
3. From friends to brethren.

417. CHRIST UNITING JEWS AND GENTILES

"He is our peace, who hath made both one, and hath broken down the middle wall of partition between us." Eph. 2:14

1. Jews and Gentiles met in his Person.
   Rahab and Ruth were among his ancestors as well as David and Mary.
2. Jews and Gentiles had a place in his ministry.
3. Jews and Gentiles are united in the church he established.

—J. Cynddylan Jones

418. CALCULATED CHRISTIANITY

"Unto me, who am less than the least of all saints, is this grace given, that I should preach among the Gentiles the unsearchable riches of Christ." Eph. 3:8

Consider how Paul calculated:

1. His condition.
   "Less than the least of all saints."
2. His resources.
   "Is this grace given."
3. His calling.
   "That I should preach."
4. His message.
   "The unsearchable riches of Christ."

—George Artingstall,
Radiant Religion

419. THE ASCENSION

"When he [Jesus] ascended on high, he led captivity captive, and gave gifts unto men." Eph. 4:8

What did the Ascension mean?

1. It meant the establishment of a new relationship.
2. It meant the recovery of a forfeited sovereignty.
3. It meant the bestowal of a new power.

—J. Gregory Mantle,
God's Tomorrow

420. HOW PAUL PREACHED SOCIAL MORALITY

"Let him that stole steal no more: but rather let him labor, working with his hands the thing which is good, that he may have to give to him that needeth." Eph. 4:28

He enjoined:

1. Honesty.
   "Let him that stole steal no more."
2. Industry.
   "But rather let him labor with his hands."
3. Property.
   "That he may have."
4. Charity.
   "To give to him that needeth."

—Henry Van Dyke (adapted)

421. THREE HUMAN TYPES

"Let him that stole steal no more: but rather let him labor, working with his hands the thing which is good, that he may have to give to him that needeth." Eph. 4:28

We have here brought before us three human types:

1. There are those who take what they do not earn. "Him that stole."
2. There are those who make that they may own. "Rather let him labor, working with his hands."
3. There are those who have that they may give. "That he may have to give." You will recall George Bernard Shaw's definition of a gentleman as one who puts more into the common pool than he takes out of it. Every Christian should be a gentleman in that sense.

422. CHRIST—THE SAVIOR OF THE BODY

"He is the saviour of the body."
Eph. 5:23

It is often said that Jesus is the savior of the soul. And that, of course, is true. But if the soul be thought of as something apart from the body, then to say that Jesus saves the soul is to state only one side of the case. Jesus is the savior not alone of the soul of man, but of the whole of man. And that includes the body.

Think of how much the Christian religion makes of the human body. No other world faith so elevates the physical part of man. Most indeed make escape from the body the goal of the religious quest.

Not so the religion of Jesus. He is the savior of the body.

How?

1. Christ saves the body from the ravages of sin.

D. H. Lawrence wished he could get rid of his body. In his poem "In Trouble and Shame" he wrote:

I wish that I could go . . .
And leave my flesh discarded lying
Like luggage of some departed traveller
Gone one knows not whither.

Then I would turn round,
And seeing my cast-off body
    lying like lumber,
I would laugh with joy.

But Christ gives us a body we can live with. He is the Savior of the body, and we shall have a body throughout all eternity.

2. Christ saves the body from the blight of disease.

Only God is the healer. "God healed me: the doctor took the fee." If God did not heal, no surgeon would dare put a knife in the human body. But God does heal. In Exod. 15:26 he introduces himself to us as the great Physician: "I am the Lord that healeth thee."

3. Christ will save the body from the dissolution of death.

Christianity teaches not only the immortality of the soul but the resurrection of the body. It says that it is not simply the spiritual part of man that survives death but the total personality, and that includes the physical organism which the soul inherits and inhabits.

PHILIPPIANS

423. THE MEANING OF LIFE

"Life means Christ to me."
Phil. 1:21 Moffatt

When Paul wrote the word "life" he spelled it with six letters thus: Christ!

What kind of life did he find in Christ?

a) Not just biological.
b) not just intellectual.
But:
c) moral and spiritual.
It was:
1. Life at its happiest.
2. Life at its highest.
3. Life at its busiest.

424. LIVING WELL

"For to me to live is Christ."
Phil. 1:21

To live well means for most people today to sup from a silver spoon or to feast on the fat of the land. But really to live well means not what one lives on so much as what one lives by and lives for.

Summing up his message, Joseph Fort Newton wrote: "My message has been very simple. It is this: to live well we must have a faith to live by, a self to live with and a work to live for."

Let us take them one by one.

1. A faith to live by.
2. A self to live with.
3. A work to live for.
Christ gives us all these.

—Quoted by G. T. Bellhouse,
in *Bread from Heaven*

425. CHRIST AND LIFE

"For to me to live is Christ."
Phil. 1:21

1. We must have some interpretation of life.
Christ supplies the clue to its meaning.
2. We must have some inspiration for life.
Christ supplies the necessary drive.
3. We must have integration of life.
Christ is the cord that holds it together.

—Robert Ferguson,
Some Reminiscences and Studies

426. THE THREE FORMS OF JESUS

The Greek word *morphe*, which occurs in each of our texts and from which we get our word *metamorphosis*, is used only three times in the New Testament, and on each occasion it is applied to our Lord Jesus Christ.

From the texts we learn that Christ had three forms:

1. The form of his divine preexistence. "Who, being in the form of God." Phil. 2:6
2. The form of his incarnate servitude. "He took upon him the form of a servant." Phil. 2:7
3. The form of his resurrection glory. "He appeared in another form unto two of them, as they walked, and went into the country." Mark 16:12

427. ABOVE EVERY NAME

"God . . . highly exalted him, and [gave] him a name which is above every name." Phil. 2:9

1. The name of Jesus is above every name in the Bible.
2. The name of Jesus is above every name in human history.
3. The name of Jesus is above every name in the church.
4. The name of Jesus must be above every other name in our personal lives.

428. THE EXALTED NAME

"God [gave] unto him a name which is above every name."
Phil. 2:9

That the name of Jesus is exalted above every other is:

1. A fact of history.
2. A spiritual necessity.
3. A personal experience.

—Henry Bett,
The Exalted Name

429. WHERE IMAGINATION FAILS

"Wherefore God also hath highly [super] exalted him." Phil. 2:9
"Where sin abounded [multiplied], grace did much more abound." Rom. 5:20

"In all these things we are more than conquerors." Rom. 8:37

Here we have:

1. A superexalted Christ.
   God also hath superexalted him.
2. A superexceeding grace.
   Grace did superabound.

3. A superexcelling Christian.
   We are superconquerors.

—Ronald A. Ward,
Royal Sacrament (adapted)

430. THE TENSION OF THE TENSES

"Brethren, I count not myself to have apprehended: but this one thing I do, forgetting those things which are behind, and reaching forth unto those things which are before, I press toward the mark for the prize of the high calling of God in Christ Jesus." Phil. 3:13, 14

The moment we hear such a sentence as this, we recognize it as the transparently honest confession of a truly great man. It is the expression of a threefold resolve.

Observe:

1. The apostle's modest valuation of the present.
   "I count not myself to have apprehended."
2. The apostle's wise resolve as to the past.
   "Forgetting those things which are behind."
3. The apostle's strenuous effort in the future.
   "I press toward the mark."

—H. O. Mackey,
Miniature Sermons

431. IMMANUEL KANT'S RECIPE FOR HAPPINESS

1. Something to do.
   "This one thing I do."
   Phil. 3:13

2. Someone to love.
"We love him, because he first loved us."
I John 4:19
3. Something to hope for.
"The Lord Jesus Christ . . . our hope." I Tim. 1:1

Footnote: Christ alone is the secret and the source of true happiness.

432. RECIPE FOR REST

"Be careful for nothing, but in every thing by prayer and supplication with thanksgiving let your requests be made known unto God. And the peace of God, which passeth all understanding, shall keep your hearts and minds through Christ Jesus."
Phil. 4:6, 7

These verses suggest:
1. That care may be destroyed.
   a) not mere carelessness.
   b) not stoical indifference.

2. That prayer may be employed.
3. That peace may be enjoyed.
—George Harper,
One Hundred Sermons in Brief

433. SAINTS IN CAESAR'S HOUSEHOLD

"All the saints salute you, chiefly they that are of Caesar's household." Phil. 4:22

What a place for saints to be in! If we were to picture white angels in hell, the contrast between character and environment could hardly be less startling!

Yet there were saints there.
1. Think of their exposure to temptation.
2. Think of the strategic position they occupied.
3. Think of what a tribute they were to the triumphant grace of God.

COLOSSIANS

434. DOES GOD FORGIVE SIN?

"In whom we have redemption through his blood, even the forgiveness of sins." Col. 1:14

There is a consciousness of sin in every man—of omission if not of wrongdoing. With this comes the conscious need of forgiveness. Is there any answer on the part of God to this need of ours?

Let us look at four answers to that question.

1. Some say that he never forgives. They maintain that moral laws are inexorable and that he who breaks them must take the consequences.
2. Some say that he forgives capriciously.
   They declare that he forgives some but declines to pardon others; that some sins are pardonable but that others are not.
3. Some say that he forgives universally, unconditionally.

161

They insist that God is too amiable and good-natured to take stern views of sin; that, in the words which Edward Fitzgerald puts upon the lips of Omar Khayyam, "He's a Good Fellow, and 'twill all be well."

4. Some say, as does Paul in the text, that God's forgiveness is based upon Christ's atoning work on the cross.

"We have redemption through his blood."

—Richard S. Storrs,
Preaching Without Notes
(adapted)

435. WHAT THE CROSS NAILS DOWN

"*Blotting out the handwriting of ordinances that was against us, which was contrary to us, and took it out of the way, nailing it to his cross.*"   Col. 2:14

There are certain concrete realities which the cross nails down for us, from which there is no possible escape.

1. One fact which the cross nails down is the grim reality of sin.
2. Another fact which the cross nails down is the agonizing cost of forgiveness.
3. A further fact which the cross nails down is the victorious purpose of God.

—Murdo Ewen Macdonald,
The Call to Obey

436. THE SUBURBAN CHRIST

"*Christ is everything and everywhere.*"   Col. 3:2

162

1. Christ is sometimes in the suburbs of our creed.
2. Christ is sometimes in the suburbs of our characters.
3. Christ is sometimes in the suburbs of our fellowship.
4. Christ is sometimes in the suburbs of our plans.

—W. J. Rowlands,
The Suburban Christ

437. ONESIMUS

"*Onesimus, a faithful and beloved brother.*"   Col. 4:9
"*My son Onesimus.*"   Phil. 10

1. What Onesimus was!
   a) a slave.
      Out of 1,600,000 people in ancient Rome, 900,000 were slaves.
   b) a criminal.
      He had stolen his master's property.
2. What he became!
   a) a freeman in Christ.
   b) a son of the apostle.
   c) a profitable servant.
3. What the power was that worked such a change in him!

"We are God's Onesimi," cried Luther, "unprofitable servants all." Yet to us at last the master may say through grace: "Well done, thou good and faithful servant."

—James Dinwoodie,
Illustrated Sermon Outlines

438. PAUL'S PAREGORICS

"*Men that have been a comfort* [Greek—*paregoria*] *unto me.*"   Col. 4:11

The word employed by the apostle in this sentence and translated "comfort" is a very interesting one. It is a term of which medical men still make use—paregoric. Paregoric is a drug that soothes the nerves and lessens pain. And here in our text Paul is telling us that there were people who for him acted as spiritual paregorics.

Let us think of some of them.

1. Ananias was one such.
   He mitigated for Paul the pain of the new birth.

2. Barnabas was another.
   He lessened for Paul the pain of suspicion.

3. Luke was yet another.
   As a physician, he may have from time to time relieved the physical pains with which the apostle appears to have been afflicted.

4. Timothy was still another.
   He allayed for Paul the pain of leaving behind the churches he had founded.

I TIMOTHY

439. IN THE SANCTUARY

"The glorious gospel of the blessed God."   I Tim. 1:11 RSV

An analysis of this sentence suggests to an imaginative mind the three parts of the ancient Hebrew tabernacle.

1. The outer court.
   "The gospel."

2. The Holy Place.
   "The glory."

3. The Holy of Holies.
   "The blessed God."

—A. E. Garvie,
A Guide to Preachers

440. PAUL GIVES HIS TESTIMONY

"I obtained mercy." I Tim. 1:13

Into these three simple transparent words Paul condensed the story of his conversion. "I obtained mercy."

What have we here?

1. The confession of a great gratitude.
   It is said that at a college celebration in Scotland, when certain medals and other distinctions were being conferred, one of the students, to the rapturous cheers of his fellows, went up to the platform to receive his honors and order. Having taken it, he went straight down to the hall and, fastening the honorable distinction on the dress of an old silver-haired woman, said with deep emotion: "Mother, that belongs rightly to you: it was your sacrifice that enabled me to win it."

2. The expression of a profound humility.

3. The utterance of a sincere repentance.

4. The declaration of an ardent love.
   In his later years, Norman

163

Macleod, of the Barony of Glasgow, wrote: "I am beginning to hate mere intellect more and more. It is clear, cold, magnificent, but, like the gleaming of a glacier —oh, so cold!"

5. The avowal of an unbounded hope for others.
"Howbeit for this cause I obtained mercy, that in me first Jesus Christ might show forth all long-suffering, for a pattern to them which should hereafter believe on him to life everlasting."
I Tim. 1:16

—H. O. Mackey,
Miniature Sermons

441. THE GOSPEL

"This is a faithful saying, and worthy of all acceptation, that Christ Jesus came into the world to save sinners." I Tim. 1:15

Consider:
1. Its contents.
   "Christ Jesus came into the world to save sinners."
2. Its credibility.
   "This is a faithful saying."
3. Its claim.
   "Worthy of all acceptation."

—B. D. Johns, *Pulpit Notes*

442. THE CHRISTIAN ATHLETE

"Exercise [gumnazo, literally gymnasticize] thyself . . . unto godliness. For bodily exercise profiteth little; but godliness is profitable unto all things, having promise of the life that now is, and of that which is to come." I Tim. 4:7, 8
"Every man that striveth for the mastery is temperate in all things. Now they do it to obtain a corruptible crown; but we an incorruptible. I therefore so run."
I Cor. 9:25, 26

1. Running clothes.
2. Athlete's food.
3. The start.
4. The race.

—George Clarke,
The Christian Athlete

443. A MINISTER'S THREE MAIN REQUIREMENTS

"Meditate upon these things; give thyself wholly to them. . . . Take heed unto thyself, and unto the doctrine." I Tim. 4:15, 16
"All Scripture is given by inspiration of God." II Tim. 3:16

1. An open book before him.
2. An open heart within him.
3. An open heaven above him.

II TIMOTHY

444. WHAT JESUS DID TO DEATH

"Christ, who hath abolished death." II Tim. 1:10

That is one of the most magnificent taunts ever flung by triumphant faith in the face of apparently falsifying facts. "Christ hath

164

abolished death." Has he? It certainly does not look like it.
And yet he *has!*
How?
1. He abolished death in his person.
2. He abolished it in his precepts.
   Other religious leaders teach their followers how to die: Christ teaches his followers how to live. Death is no part of his program for them.
3. He will abolish it in his people.
   As he rose, so we shall rise.

445. THE MAN WHO KNOWS

"I know whom I have believed."
II Tim. 1:12

There are, broadly speaking, four sorts of men:
1. The man who knows not, and knows not that he knows not.
   He is a fool—shun him!
2. The man who knows not, and knows that he knows not.
   He is simple—teach him!
3. The man who knows, and knows not that he knows.
   He is asleep—wake him!
4. The man who knows, and knows that he knows.
   He is wise—follow him!
Paul belonged to this last-named category.

446. HONORABLE VESSELS

"If a man therefore purge himself from these, he shall be a vessel

unto honor, sanctified, and meet for the master's use, and prepared unto every good work."
II Tim. 2:21

Christ, as head of the church, is master of a great house. In that house many vessels are in use. Some of us, like vessels of coarse material and rude workmanship, can serve only a mean and passing purpose. Others are of greater value and are fit for higher service.
Note that:
1. The composition of the honorable vessels fits them for the master's use.
   What shall be done with the various vessels is settled, so far, by what they are made of.
2. The conformation of the honorable vessels fits them for the master's use.
   The service to which a vessel may be put depends very much on its shape and size and ornamentation.
3. The consecration of the honorable vessels fits them for the master's use.
   It is for the owner to determine their office, set them apart to it, and reserve them for it.

—David Burns,
Sayings in Symbol

447. THE TEMPTATIONS OF A MINISTER

(An Ordination Sermon)

"The servant of the Lord must not. . . ."
II Tim. 2:24

1. The temptation to recline.
   To take things easy.

165

2. The temptation to shine.
To show off.
3. The temptation to whine.
To grumble at his lot.

—David Christie,
The Service of Christ

448. LEFT LUGGAGE

"The cloak which I left at Troas with Carpus, when thou comest, bring with thee, and the books, but especially the parchments."
II Tim. 4:13

Of what did Paul's left luggage consist?

1. Provision for his physical need.
"The cloak."

2. Provision for his intellectual need.
"The books."
3. Provision for his spiritual need.
"The parchments."

449. COME BEFORE WINTER

"Do thy diligence to come before winter." II Tim. 4:21

1. Come to Christ before the winter of doubt sets in.
2. Come to Christ before the winter of sorrow breaks upon you.
3. Come to Christ before the winter of death deprives you of the chance of coming.

TITUS

450. ENTERING THE SCHOOL OF CHRIST

Tit. 2:10-14; 3:5-7

1. The master we meet.
"The grace of God that bringeth salvation hath appeared." Tit. 2:11
2. The lessons we learn.
"Denying ungodliness and worldly lusts, we should live soberly, righteously, and godly, in this present world."
Tit. 2:12
3. The career we await.
"Looking for that blessed hope, and the glorious appearing of the great God and our Saviour Jesus Christ."
Tit. 2:13

4. The uniform we wear.
"Who gave himself for us, that he might . . . purify unto himself a peculiar people, zealous of good works."
Tit. 2:14

—John Wood,
The Preacher's Workshop

451. THE HIGHEST ART AND HOW TO MASTER IT

"The grace of God that bringeth salvation hath appeared to all men, teaching us that, denying ungodliness and worldly lusts, we should live soberly, righteously, and godly, in this present world."
Tit. 2:11, 12

The gospel teaches us to live in relation to three worlds:

1. The world within us.
   "Soberly."
2. The world around us.

"Righteously."

3. The world above us.
   "Godly."

—J. A. Evans,
One Hundred Sermons in Brief

PHILEMON

452. A SOUL'S TRAGEDY

"*Demas . . . my fellow-laborer.*"
Philem. 24

"*Demas.*"   Col. 4:14

"*Demas hath forsaken me, having loved this present world.*"
II Tim. 4:10

1. Entity.
   A man with a contribution to make.
2. Identity.
   A mere name.
3. Nonentity.
   Demas disappears from history, "having loved this present world."

HEBREWS

453. THE THREEFOLD MINISTRY OF CHRIST

"*God, having of old time spoken unto the fathers in the prophets by divers portions and in divers manners, hath at the end of these days spoken unto us in His Son, whom He appointed heir of all things, through whom also He made the worlds; who being the effulgence of His glory, and the very image of His substance, and upholding all things by the word of His power, when He had made purification of sins, sat down on the right hand of the Majesty on high.*"   Heb. 1:1-3

1. Christ as prophet.
   "God . . . hath in these last days spoken unto us by his Son."   Heb. 1:1
2. Christ as priest.
   "Who, when he had by himself purged our sins."
   Heb. 1:3
3. Christ as king.
   "Sat down on the right hand of the Majesty on high."
   Heb. 1:3

—Andrew Murray,
The Holiest of All

454. JESUS, KING MOST WONDERFUL

"*We see Jesus . . . crowned.*"
Heb. 2:9

167

1. When we look backward, we see Jesus crowned on the cross.
2. When we look upward, we see Jesus crowned in heaven.
3. When we look onward, we see Jesus crowned on the earth.
4. When we look inward, we see Jesus crowned in our hearts.

—Geoffrey R. King,
Truth for Our Time

455. THE ABILITY OF CHRIST

"He is able." Heb. 2:18

1. He is able . . . to save.
   Heb. 7:25
2. He is able to keep.
   Jude 24; II Tim. 1:12
3. He is able to perfect.
   Jude 24; Acts 20:32

—James Dinwoodie,
Illustrated Sermon Outlines

456. THE HOUSE OF JESUS CHRIST

"Whose house are we."
Heb. 3:6

During his earthly ministry, Jesus had no house to call his own. His foster-father Joseph provided a house for him in Nazareth when he was a lad, and his heavenly Father had a house waiting for him when he left this world, but while Jesus was engaged in his life-work here, he had no house to call his own!

Yet here is the writer to the Hebrews speaking of a house that belongs to Jesus—the church—and he says that the church is a house which Christ possesses. Observe that there are three ways of becoming an owner:

1. By purchase.
   We may pay the market price for it. Jesus bought his church. "Ye are bought with a price." I Cor. 6:20
2. By production.
   When we ourselves make a thing, it belongs to us by right. Jesus is building his church. "I will build my church." Matt. 16:18
3. By virtue of a will.
   We may inherit property. Jesus has acquired the church by the gift of his heavenly Father. "Thine they were, and thou gavest them me." John 17:6

—W. Price,
Sketches of Sermons

457. THE WORD OF GOD

"For the word of God is quick, and powerful, and sharper than any two-edged sword, piercing even to the dividing asunder of soul and spirit, and of the joints and marrow, and is a discerner of the thoughts and intents of the heart."
Heb. 4:12

According to our text, the word of God is:

1. Vital.
   "Quick."
2. Potential.
   "Powerful."
3. Surgical.
   "'Sharper than any two-edged sword."

Dr. David Livingstone records that the Africans known as the Bechuanas are excellent patients. In any operation, even the women sat unmoved. In cutting out a tumour one inch in diameter, he has known them to sit and talk as though they felt nothing. Yet when the word of God has been preached to these same people in the power of the Spirit of God, they have had to run away from the church building lest their tears should be seen by their fellow men and women.

4. Psychoanalytical.
"And is a discerner of the thoughts and intents of the heart."

—George Cumming
(adapted)

458. THE DIVINE X-RAY

"All things are naked and opened unto the eyes of him with whom we have to do." Heb. 4:13

Observe that:
1. God sees all our secret sins.
2. God sees all our buried sorrows.
3. God sees all our hidden motives.

459. JESUS CHRIST— AUTHOR

"The author of eternal salvation."
Heb. 5:9

Jesus is referred to in our text as being an author. We usually associate the term with a writer of books. Jesus never wrote a book. Hence when the writer to the Hebrews referred to Jesus as an author, he was using the term in a very wide and elastic sense.

Yet there are four books of which Jesus is the author:
1. The Book of Nature.
2. The Book of Conscience.
3. The Book of Divine Purposes.
4. The Book of Salvation.

—J. Price Williams,
All Clear

460. CHRIST'S ABILITY TO SAVE

"He is able . . . to save."
Heb. 7:25

He is able to save:
1. From irrationality.
He makes sense of this ambiguous world.
2. From immorality.
He redeems this sinful world.
3. From mortality.
He offers life to this dying world.

461. THREE NEW TESTAMENT SLOGANS

1. Once for all—the gospel's finished work.
"Christ was once offered to bear the sins of many."
Heb. 9:28
2. All or nothing—the gospel's total demand.
"Sell all that thou hast, and distribute unto the poor."
Luke 18:22
3. Now or never—the gospel's imperious challenge.
"Behold, now is the accepted time; behold, now is the day of salvation."
II Cor. 6:2
—W. R. Maltby

169

462. THE THREE GREAT EMBODIMENTS OF THE HOLY SPIRIT

"A body hast thou prepared me."
Heb. 10:5
"All Scripture . . . given by inspiration of God . . . is profitable for doctrine. . . ." II Tim 3:16
"For by one Spirit are we all baptized into one body."
I Cor. 12:13

1. The embodiment of the eternal Spirit in a Man.
   The incarnation of the Word.
2. The embodiment of the eternal Spirit in a Book.
   The inspiration of the Word.
3. The embodiment of the eternal Spirit in the church.
   The integration of the Word.

463. THE HANDS OF GOD

"Into the hands." Heb. 10:31
"On the hands." Isa. 49:16
"Under the hands." I Pet. 5:6

Has God got hands, then? Has he limbs with manual appendages like ours, frameworks of bone, infused with blood, covered with skin? No, of course not! God has no hands. He is not physical. He is spiritual. "God," said Jesus, "is Spirit." He has no body with parts and passions, organs and functions. He has no hands.

And yet here is the Bible distinctly and definitely telling us that he does have hands! What does it mean? It is speaking symbolically, using a figure of speech, and what it intends to convey is that he is a God who does things, a God who acts.

170

Think of three biblical references to the hands of God .

1. The terrible hands of judgment.
   "It is a fearful thing to fall into the hands of the living God." Heb. 10:31
   Somebody has said that it would be a far more fearful thing to fall out of them. We don't know. Certainly we cannot endorse or approve the awful language used by Jonathan Edwards in a sermon preached at Enfield, Connecticut, on July 8, 1741. He spoke of: "The God that holds you over the pit of hell, much as one holds a spider or other loathsome insect over the fire." We cannot, I say, endorse that; but neither can we ignore or minimize the dreadful fact of divine judgment.
2. The tender hands of love.
   "Behold, I have graven thee upon the palms of my hands."
   Isa. 49:16

   Sings Augustus Toplady:

   My name from the palms of His hands
   Eternity will not erase;
   Impressed on His heart it remains,
   In marks of indelible grace.

3. The tremendous hands of power.
   "Humble yourselves . . . under the mighty hand of God." I Pet. 5:6
   More than anything we need nowadays to experience "the mighty ordination of the piercéd hands."

464. WHAT FAITH IN GOD CAN DO

(As illustrated in Heb. 11.)

1. It can perceive the invisible. "He endured, as seeing him who is invisible."
Heb. 11:27
2. It can believe the incredible. "Through faith we understand that the worlds were framed by the word of God."
Heb. 11:3
3. It can achieve the impossible. "Time would fail me to tell of [those] who through faith subdued kingdoms, wrought righteousness, obtained promises, stopped the mouths of lions, quenched the violence of fire." Heb. 11:32-34

465. THE FAITH OF MOSES

"By faith Moses, when he was come to years, refused to be called the son of Pharaoh's daughter; choosing rather to suffer affliction with the people of God, than to enjoy the pleasures of sin for a season. . . . By faith . . . he endured, as seeing him who is invisible . . . he had respect unto the recompense of the reward."
Heb. 11:24-25, 27, 26

We have here:

1. Faith's refusal. "Moses . . . refused."
2. Faith's realization. "Seeing him who is invisible."
3. Faith's reward. "He had respect unto the recompense of the reward."

466. SEEING THE INVISIBLE

"By faith he [Moses] forsook Egypt, not fearing the wrath of the king: for he endured, as seeing him who is invisible." Heb. 11:27

1. The vision of faith. "Seeing him."
2. The venture of faith. "He forsook."
3. The valor of faith. "He endured."

—N. A. Ross,
Seeing the Invisible

467. HOLDING ON TO THE INVISIBLE

"He endured, as seeing him who is invisible." Heb. 11:27

There is a fine verse in the Epistle to the Hebrews which is most suggestively translated in Luther's version: "He held on to him whom he saw not, as though he saw him."
Reflect that:

1. We must do this in relation to the ultimate ambiguity and mystery of things.
2. We must do this in connection with our personal sorrows.
3. We must do this in our life of private devotion.

468. CHRIST THE FINISHER

"The finisher of our faith."
Heb. 12:2

There is always a peculiar satisfaction in finishing a thing. The architect knows it when he sees his dream materialize in stone or steel; the artist knows it when he contemplates some completed canvas on which he has lavished the labor of years; the author knows it when he holds in his hands a monumental volume in which is distilled the thought and experience of a lifetime. Yes, there is certainly a peculiar satisfaction in finishing a thing.

Now the New Testament describes our Lord as "the finisher of our faith"—the one who is going to bring our believing to full flowering and fruition.

This is one of Christ's distin-guishing characteristics—he never leaves a job half done.

Consider that:

1. He was the finisher of creation.
   "He spake, and it was done; he commanded, and it stood fast." Ps. 33:9
2. He was the finisher of salvation.
   "It is finished." John 19:30
3. He will be the finisher of the restoration.
   "Through him to reconcile all things unto himself." Col. 1:20

JAMES

469. THE POWER OF SIN

"Sin, when it is finished, bringeth forth death." James 1:15

Consider:

1. Its deceiving power.
2. Its self-betraying power.
3. Its separating power.
4. Its enslaving power.
5. Its propagating power.
6. Its deadening power.

—John R. Mott, in
The Secret of Preaching Power

470. A MIRROR FOR THE SOUL

"For if any be a hearer of the word . . . he is like unto a man beholding his natural face in a glass." James 1:23

Man has an innate curiosity about himself. The mirror helps him to see what his body is like.

But his interest in himself is not merely "skin deep." He is curious about his soul. Is there a mirror of the soul? There is. It is the Bible.

Consider that:

1. The Bible reveals the origin of the soul.
2. The Bible reveals the ills of the soul.
3. The Bible reveals the destiny of the soul.
   How must we use this mirror?
   a) Frequently and regularly.
   b) Skillfully.

—Rupert Clinton Foster,
The Everlasting Gospel

471. THE MEANING OF LIFE

"What is your life?" James 4:14

What is life?

1. It is a gift.
2. It is an opportunity.
3. It is a beginning.

—E. D. Jarvis,
If Any Man Minister

472. DOES PRAYER CHANGE ANYTHING?

"*The effectual fervent prayer of a righteous man availeth much.*"
James 5:16

1. It changes me.
2. It changes the atmosphere of a home in such a way as to affect the lives of the entire family.
3. It opens doors into the unseen order which enfolds us all.

—Charles R. Brown

473. PRAYER AND EFFICIENCY

"*The effectual fervent prayer of a righteous man availeth much in its working.*"
James 5:16

1. Prayer does something in us.
2. Prayer does something for us.
3. Prayer does something through us.

—Charles Frederick Wishart,
The God of the Unexpected

I PETER

474. THE LIVING STONE

"*To whom coming as unto a living stone.*"
I Pet. 2:4

Observe that:

1. Christ is the lodestone to draw us.
2. Christ is the touchstone to test us.
3. Christ is the cornerstone to support us.

—David Burns, *God's Poem*

475. LIVING STONES

"*To whom coming, as unto a living stone, disallowed indeed of men, but chosen of God, and precious, ye also, as lively stones, are built up a spiritual house.*"
I Pet. 2:4, 5

Simon seems to have had stones very much on his mind ever since that day at Caesarea-Philippi when Jesus had renamed him "Peter," "petros," a stone.

He was not so foolish or infatuated as to suppose that he himself was the stone on which the church was to be built. "To whom coming," he says, not "to me" but "to Christ, as unto a living stone."

Then he goes on to compare his fellow-Christians to living stones.

Three thoughts are suggested by the language he uses in this connection.

1. Vitality.
    "Living stones."
    "Dead as a stone" is an idiom we sometimes use. But these stones are living. Some think the apostle was referring to magnetic stones.

173

2. Stability.
   When David Livingstone died in Central Africa, his body was carried by African bearers six hundred miles to the coast and transported to England, later to be buried in Westminster Abbey. On the occasion of the funeral, Mr. Punch, Britain's national jester, laid aside for once his bauble, cap, and bells, and to the memory of the famous missionary paid this noble tribute: "Let marble crumble, this is *Livingstone!*"
3. Symmetry.
   "Ye also are built up a spiritual house."
   You cannot build a temple with unhewn stone. Stones for the sanctuary must be chiseled into shapeliness.

476. THE PRECIOUSNESS OF CHRIST

"*Unto you therefore which believe he is precious.*"   I Pet. 2:7

Things are precious, in the main, for three reasons:

1. Because of their rarity.
   Christ is not only rare, he is unique.
2. Because of their intrinsic worth.
   Christ's infinite worthship entitles him to eternal worship.
3. Because of their purchasing power.
   Christ, with his blood, paid the price of our redemption.

477. WHAT CHRIST THE CARPENTER HAS MADE OF HIS CROSS

"*Who his own self bare our sins in his body on the tree.*"
I Pet. 2:24

What do you see when you look at a tree? That depends, to a great degree, upon who and what you are. A carpenter looks at a tree and in it he sees so much timber, capable of being manufactured by his craftsmanship into certain articles of joinery. A botanist looks at a tree and he immediately classifies it as oak, beech, birch, poplar, sycamore, cypress, and so on. A poet looks at a tree and, as he does so, its beauty causes his soul to burst into song. That, you may recall, was what happened to Joyce Kilmer. He has a charming little lyric called "Trees" in which he enshrines his emotions during such arboreal contemplation.

I need not remind you that Christ was a carpenter, and that a carpenter is a worker in wood; and I would like you to notice what Christ the carpenter has made of the wood of his cross.

He has made of it:

1. A balance in which to weigh the worth of the human soul.
2. A coffin in which to bury sin forever.
3. A ladder by which a sinful soul may scale the skies.
4. A throne from which he dominates the ages.
5. A table to which he graciously invites his guests.

478. THE TREE

"Who his own self bare our sins in his own body on the tree."
I Pet. 2:24

It is eminently fitting that the cross should be spoken of as a tree. Here are three reasons for the aptitude of the figure:

1. A tree is something which can bring down lightning from heaven.
   At the cross God's judgment flashed forth against sin.
2. A tree is something which defies time.
   The oldest living things in the world are trees.
3. A tree is something which is used for constructive purposes.
   With the timber of his cross Christ is building his church.

479. THE FAITHFULNESS OF GOD

"Let them that suffer according to the will of God commit the keeping of their souls to him in well doing, as unto a faithful Creator."   I Pet. 4:19

Notice that:

1. God is faithful in his promises.
2. God is faithful in his providences.
3. God is faithful in his punishments.

480. TEACHING BY ONE'S MISTAKES

We are all familiar with the concept of learning by our mistakes. But the process may with profit be carried a stage further. We can not only learn, but *teach,* by our mistakes; and so others, if they heed us, may be spared the costly errors into which we have inadvertently fallen.

Peter did that. He taught by his mistakes.

First, think of three of his greatest faults and then observe how he warned others against them.

1. Hotheadedness.
   That was Peter's biggest fault. No fewer than three times in his epistles, as Moffatt translates them, did the apostle admonish his readers: "Keep cool."
2. Pride.
   This was another of Peter's faults. He had a very high opinion of himself, "fancied his chance," as people say. But notice how in his first epistle, he uses a most expressive term reminiscent of a never-to-be-forgotten scene in the life of his Lord: "Be towelled with humility."
   I Pet. 5:5
3. Busybodyism.
   This was the third fault to which Peter was addicted. He was, to employ a colloquialism, "nosey," interfering, a meddler in other people's affairs. An instance of it is found in John 21:21: "Lord, and what shall this man do?" Later, Peter wrote: "Let none of you suffer as a murderer, or as a thief, or an evildoer, or as a busybody in other men's matters."
   I Pet. 4:15

175

II PETER

481. THE THREE VOICES

"There came such a voice to him from the excellent glory."
II Pet. 1:17
"We have also a more sure word of prophecy." II Pet. 1:19
"No prophecy of the Scripture is of any private interpretation."
II Pet. 1:20

Peter is an old man. He is in reminiscent mood, dwelling in the past, as is the manner of old men. His master has told him that he has not long to live. "Knowing that the putting off of my tabernacle cometh swiftly, even as our Lord Jesus Christ signified unto me." So he writes. "Tabernacle!" The word evokes memories. He remembers an hour when he wanted to build three tabernacles on the snow-crowned crest of Hermon. Then he recalls the three voices, and it is about these that I want to speak.

1. The voice from the heavens.
2. The voice from the lips.
3. The voice from the Book.

482. SPIRITUAL MATURATION

"Grow in grace." II Pet. 3:18

1. The Christian should grow downward.
His life should be marked by increasing depth.
2. The Christian should grow upward.
His life should be characterized by continual aspiration.
3. The Christian should grow inward.
His life should be noted for progressing holiness.
4. The Christian should grow outward.
His life should be conspicuous for zeal in service.

—Paul E. Holdcraft,
Snappy Sermon Starters

I JOHN

483. THE GIST OF THE GOSPEL

"That which was from the beginning, which we have heard, which we have seen with our eyes, which we have looked upon, and our hands have handled, of the Word of life . . . That which we have seen and heard declare we unto you." I John 1:1, 3
Here we have set before us the gist of the gospel.

Note that:

1. It is something eternal.
"That which was from the beginning."
2. It is something historical.
"That which we have heard, which we have seen with our eyes . . . and our hands have handled."
3. It is something homiletical.
"That . . . declare we unto you."

176

484. GOD AND LIGHT

Here is a catena of biblical passages which presents to my mind a brilliant picture—a picture of:

1. The sun.
"God is light." I John 1:5
"Who only hath immortality, dwelling in the light which no man can approach unto."
I Tim. 6:16
Scientists today are planning to put a man on the moon: they will never dream of putting a man on the sun—not just because of its distance from the earth but because of the intensity of its heat. It is indeed unapproachable. So God is in his eternal being.

2. The ray.
"I am the light of the world."
John 8:12
Christ is the sunlight who came to the world as the sun itself could never come.

3. The torches.
"Ye are the light of the world." Matt. 5:14
"Ye shine as lights in the world." Phil. 2:15
The true Christian is a flaming torch lit by the beam of Christ with the fire of God's sun.

O Light that followest all my way,
I yield my flickering torch to thee;
My heart restores its borrowed ray,
That in thy sunshine's blaze its day
May brighter, fairer be.
—George Matheson

485. THE LIVING LIGHT

1. The sun.
"God is light, and in him is no darkness at all."
I John 1:5
"Who only hath immortality, dwelling in the light which no man can approach unto."
I Tim. 6:16

2. The sunshine.
"I am the light of the world."
John 8:12

3. The lamps.
"Ye are the light of the world." Matt. 5:14
"Among whom ye shine as lights in the world."
Phil. 2:15

486. THE BIRTHMARKS OF A CHRISTIAN

I John 2:3; 3:14; 3:24

To an address on these three texts an old preacher gave the arresting title "The Birthmarks of a Christian."

Natural birthmarks are blemishes: spiritual birthmarks are beauty spots. A natural birthmark is a purple pigmentation of the skin: a spiritual birthmark represents salvation from sin.

Examine the Christian's birthmarks:

1. The law that he keeps.
"Hereby we do know that we know him, if we keep his commandments."
I John 2:3

2. The love that he shows.
"We know that we have passed from death unto life, because we love the brethren." I John 3:14

3. The life that he shares.
"Hereby we know that he

177

abideth in us, by the Spirit which he hath given us."

I John 3:24

487. WHY CHRIST WAS MANIFESTED

1. To destroy the works of the devil.
   "For this purpose the Son of God was manifested, that he might destroy the works of the devil." I John 3:8
2. To take away our sins.
   "Ye know that he was manifested to take away our sins."
   I John 3:5
3. To reveal the Father.
   "He that hath seen me hath seen the Father."
   John 14:9
4. To prepare for a Second Advent.
   "Christ was once offered to bear the sins of many; and unto them that look for him shall he appear the second time without sin unto salvation." Heb. 9:28

—G. Campbell Morgan

488. THE ACID TEST

"We know that we have passed from death unto life, because we love the brethren." I John 3:14

"We know that we have passed from death unto life, because we love"—whom? Our enemies? That is indeed a searching test. Our neighbors? That, too, can be a critical trial. But—our brothers? That, if you will not misunderstand me, is in some senses the hardest thing of all.

Why?
1. Ancestry has something to do with it.
   Notice how Christ brings out in his parables contrasts between brothers. That is likewise the motif of such works as *The Brothers Karamazov* by Dostoevski, *Master of Ballantrae* by Robert Louis Stevenson, *The Brothers*, by L. A. C. Strong, and so on. But surely the spiritual ancestry of the sons of God should make it easy for them to love one another!
2. Proximity has something to do with it.
   I meet my brother a thousand times for every once I meet a stranger, a hundred times perhaps for every twice I meet my neighbor. That can make it hard to love him.
3. Rivalry has something to do with it.
   Reinhold Niebuhr has pointed out the special difficulties we all have in getting on with foes and competitors. Brothers are usually competitors and that makes love hard. Hard—but far from impossible! Indeed the apostle makes the possession of such brotherly love the proof that we "have passed from death unto life."

They questioned my theology,
And talked of modern thought:
Bade me recite a dozen creeds—
I could not as I ought.

"I've but one creed," I answer made,
"And do not want another:
I know I've passed from death to life
Because I love my brother."

178

489. CHRISTIANS IN THE WORLD

"As he [Jesus] is, so are we in this world." I John 4:17

And what was Christ's position in the world?

1. He was a stranger in it.
   "He was in the world, and the world was made by him, and the world knew him not." John 1:10
2. He was a "failure" in it.
   "From that time many of his disciples went back, and walked no more with him." John 6:66
3. He was the supreme victor over it.
   "I have overcome the world." John 16:33

—J. Ithel Jones,
Temple and Town

490. IDOLS IN THE MODERN WORLD

"Little children, keep yourselves from idols." I John 5:21

This piece of apostolic advice may well seem utterly obsolete and irrelevant to people living in our sophisticated civilization where so many do not even believe in the true God, let alone the false ones. "Keep yourselves from idols." Such counsel might have been suitable enough for John's first readers, or for the pagans in our modern world, but where we are concerned it is totally impertinent. It simply doesn't apply. We don't bow down to wood and stone or mentally invest mere things with the attributes of life.

No! of course, we don't! Or— do we? Are all the idols gone? Here are three that are still with us.

1. Mammon.
   God of money.
2. Aphrodite.
   Goddess of sex.
3. Mars.
   God of war.

III JOHN

491. A HEALTHY-MINDED RELIGION

"Beloved, I wish above all things that thou mayest prosper and be in health, even as thy soul prospereth." III John 2

Here is a reference to religion with health at its heart. We do not believe in the so-called "religion of healthy-mindedness," but we do most emphatically believe in the healthy-mindedness of true religion.

Consider the healthy-mindedness of Christianity.

1. It is healthy-minded because it is rooted in the great objectivities of history.
   "Regaled myself," wrote Thomas Chalmers, "with the solidity of the objective facts of religion."
   "Wise counsellors," remarks D. M. Baillie, "tell us to turn away from our own feelings to the objective reali-

179

ties of our faith." Some years ago there appeared in the *British Weekly* an account of the following incident in the childhood of General Booth. A quaint old Methodist said to the little boy: "Willie Booth, do you know that your religion is something that comes to you from outside of you?" The editor, in commenting upon the question, says that that definition, crude as it is, is true to the picture of religion given in the Bible. Throughout the Book, he declares, "religion, and the support which religion gives, is something that comes from outside or above us, something that has its roots and tributaries in margins that lie beyond the personality."

2. It is healthy-minded because of its social concern.

The gospel turns *others* into *brothers.*
As Archbishop Coggan expresses it: "The Christian faith views man not as a *soul* but as a *whole.*"

3. It is healthy-minded because it organizes itself into a community.
According to Professor Alfred North Whitehead, "Religion is what a man does with his solitariness." According to John Wesley, "Christianity knows nothing of a solitary religion." Religion must begin in the soul, but if it ends in the soul it has never really begun.

4. It is healthy-minded because it teaches the practice of prayer.
In his *Primitive Physic* John Wesley speaks of "that grand old-fashioned medicine, prayer." It is more than medicine: it is health.

JUDE

492. THE FINALITY OF THE FAITH

"It was needful for me to write unto you, and exhort you that ye should earnestly contend for the faith which was once delivered unto the saints." Jude 3

Of this final faith I bid you notice that:

1. It was not discovered by human research.
2. It was not devised by human ingenuity.

3. It was delivered by divine revelation.

493. SIN IS LIKE FIRE
"Pulling them out of the fire." Jude 23

The thing spoken of here is sin. The thing used to represent it is fire.

Notice some of the resemblances between them.

1. Sin, like fire, is mysterious.
2. Sin, like fire, has power to attract.

3. Sin, like fire, has power to destroy.
   a) It destroys without regard to the worth of what it consumes.
   b) It destroys all if left to itself.
   c) It consumes quickly.
4. Sin, like fire, can be put out. Sings Charles Wesley:

I want an even strong desire,
  I want a calmly fervent zeal,
To save poor souls out of the fire,
  To snatch them from the verge of hell,
And turn them to the pardoning God.
And quench the brands in Jesus' blood.

REVELATION

494. THE ENCHANTED ISLE

"I . . . was in the isle. . . . I was in the Spirit." Rev. 1:9, 10

Here we have a story of two environments—the one an inhospitable rock, dreary and desolate; the other a celestial world, radiant with heavenly companionships.
The text suggests six contrasts:
1. The contrast between the visible and the invisible.
2 The contrast between choice and compulsion.
3. The contrast between solitude and society.
4. The contrast between circumstance and character.
5. The contrast between trouble and trust.
6. The contrast between separation and union.

—E. H. Hobday, *Calvary Clover*

495. THE TENSES OF CHRIST'S TIME

"I am he that liveth, and was dead; and, behold, I am alive for evermore." Rev. 1:18

1. The yesterday of Christ. "And was dead."
2. The today of Christ. "I am he that liveth."
3. The tomorrow of Christ. "And, behold, I am alive for evermore."

—J. S. Morgan, *One Hundred Sermons in Brief*

496. GOD'S ADVERTISEMENT

"Buy of me." Rev. 3:18

1. The merchant.
   He trades with us:
   a) personally.
      "me."
   b) singly.
      "I counsel *thee*."
   c) kindly.
      "I counsel [not compel] thee."
2. The goods.
3. The customers.

—B. D. Johns, *Pulpit Notes*

497. CHRIST AT THE DOOR

"Behold, I stand at the door, and knock: if any man hear my voice,

and open the door, I will come in to him, and will sup with him, and he with me." Rev. 3:20

Here we see:

1. Christ's attitude.
   "Behold, I stand at the door."
   "Christ stands at the door," says Samuel Chadwick. "He does not sit on the doorstep, nor on anything less than a throne."
2. Christ's appeal.
   "If any man hear my voice, and open the door."
3. Christ's assurance.
   "I will come in to him, and will sup with him, and he with me."

—A. E. Garvie,
A Guide to Preachers

498. CHRIST AT THE DOOR

"Behold, I stand at the door." Rev. 3:20

Keble College, Oxford, houses the original painting by Holman Hunt entitled "The Light of the World." As all the world knows, the painting depicts Jesus, a crowned and bejewelled figure, standing outside a brier-covered, handleless door, a lighted lantern in one hand, the other hand knocking gently for admittance.

A father and his small son were looking at that picture one day, when the boy suddenly asked: "Daddy, why don't they let him in?" Then, before his father had time to reply, the lad answered his own question: "I expect it's because they live in the basement and can't hear him!"

182

That picture of Christ at the door appeals powerfully to the imagination. It suggests four thoughts to a reflective mind.

1. The thought of courtesy.
   The house of the human heart belongs to Jesus, but he will not burgle his way into it. He waits to be admitted.
2. The thought of dignity.
   He stands: He does not sit.
3. The thought of charity.
   It is love that makes him thus linger at the entrance to that lowly dwelling.
4. The thought of urgency.
   He is standing—a posture of impermanence—and he may move away! Let him in now!

499. THE DIMENSIONS OF THE CHURCH

"Rise, and measure the temple of God." Rev. 11:1

1. What are the depths of the church?
   How far down does it go?
   a) in doctrine?
   b) in devotion?
   c) to reach those in distress?
2. What is the breadth of the church?
   Has it true catholicity? How broad is it:
   a) in doctrine?
   b) in all-inclusive fellowship?
3. What is the height of the church?
   How lofty are its ideals, its aspirations?

—Unknown

500. THE LAMB

"The Lamb slain from the foundation of the world." Rev. 13:8
"Behold, the Lamb of God, which taketh away the sin of the world!" John 1:29

"After this I beheld, and lo, a great multitude, which no man could number, of all nations, and kindreds, and people, and tongues, stood before the throne, and before the Lamb." Rev. 7:9

Every great people has its national symbol. The symbol of the United States is the eagle; the symbol of Great Britain is the lion; the symbol of Russia is the bear; the symbol of China is the dragon.

Now the kingdom of God, too, has its national symbol. But it is not a ferocious bird or savage animal, real or imaginary. It is a Lamb, the Lamb of God.

Consider:

1. The Lamb slain from the foundation of the world. First text.
2. The Lamb slain for the salvation of the world. Second text.
3. The Lamb slain as the adoration of the world. Third text.

501. THE AFFIRMATIVE SPIRIT

"Yea, saith the Spirit." Rev. 14:13

The Spirit says "Yes" to the:

1. Person of God.
2. Promises of God.
3. Power of God.
4. Plan of God.

502. HOW THE THIEF COMES

"Behold, I come as a thief." Rev. 16:15

1. He comes at the darkest part of the night.
2. He comes quietly and unobserved by sleepers.
3. He comes to snatch something.
4. He is after jewels and gold and pearls.
5. He is not interested in things of no value.
6. He has come and gone before others are aware of it.
7. He leaves the house greatly impoverished and himself greatly enriched.

—M. R. DeHaan,
The Second Coming of Jesus

503. THE MORNING STAR

"I am the . . . morning star." Rev. 22:16

This implies that:

1. Christ's influence is as light after darkness.
2. Christ's influence possesses for ever the freshness of the dawn.
3. Christ's influence is the pledge of a glorious future.
4. Christ's influence is the harbinger of eternal day.

—William Garden Blaikie,
For the Work of the Ministry
(adapted)

ACKNOWLEDGMENTS

The author expresses appreciation to the following for permission to outline these sermons:

Abingdon Press for "The Love of God," from *Getting to Know God* by John A. Redhead; "Three Types of Ministers" and "'Does Prayer Change Anything?" from *In the Minister's Workshop* by Halford Luccock; "Loyalty to God in Human Relations," "Your Soul Under the Searchlight," "The Parable of the Soils," "A Man's Religion in Terms of Building," and "The Ideal Church for Today" from *Expository Preaching for Today* by Andrew W. Blackwood; "Man's Wrath Praising God," "Divine Dealings," "Ants," "Spiritual Maturation" from *Snappy Sermon Starters* by Paul E. Holdcraft; "Christ's Gift of Restfulness," "The Voice That Quiets Your Fears," "The Riches of Christ," "A New Beginning" from *Doctrinal Preaching for Today* by Andrew W. Blackwood; "The Transfiguration of Ambition" from *Preaching* by Walter Russell Bowie; "Three Philosophies of Life" from *What Is a Christian?* by A. Leonard Griffith; "A Threefold Contrast" from *Anointed to Preach* by Clovis G. Chappell; "Christ as the Master of Time" from *Sangster's Special-Day Sermons* by W. E. Sangster; "The Heresy of Living in Compartments," "What Is Your View of Religion?" "The Magnetism of Christ," "A Gospel to Be Proud of" from *The Vitality of Faith* by Murdo E. Macdonald.

B. McCall Barbour for "Thorns" from *Lectures to Young Preachers* by George Henderson.

Carey Kingsgate Press for "The Upturned Look," "Filled with the Holy Ghost," "Intoxication," and "Christians in the World" from *Temple and Town* by J. Ithel Jones.

T. & T. Clark for "The Door of Faith" by H. A. Hammerton, from *The Expository Times;* "The Advocate" by James Stalker from *Sub Corona.*

James Clarke & Co. for sermon outlines from *One Hundred Illustrated Outlines and Texts* by James Dinwoodie; *Springs of Water* by Douglas M. Joss; *The Secret of a Warm Heart* by Norman McLeod Caie; *The Virtue of Gladness* by Bernard J. Snell; *Illustrated Sermon Outlines* by James Dinwoodie; *God's Poem* by David Burns; *The Untroubled Heart* by John A. Duke; *Faith and Progress* by H. Maldwyn Hughes.

Dehoff Publications for "A Mirror for the Soul" by Rupert Clinton Foster from *The Everlasting Gospel.*

William B. Eerdmans Publishing Company for "Mary's Memorial of Devotion" from *Preaching and Biblical Theology* by Edmund P. Clowney; "The Power of Sin" from *The Secret of Preaching Power* by Simon Blocker; "Wanting the Impossible," "The Sin of Inactivity," "At His Feet," and "The Discipline of Disappointment" from *Wanting the Impossible* by George B. Duncan; "Jesus, King Most Wonderful" from *Truth for Our Time* by Geoffrey R. King; "The Blessings of the New Birth," from *Enter into Life* by William Fitch. Used by permission.

Epworth Press for sermon outlines from *Radiant Religion* by George Artingstall; *The Three Half-Moons* by F. W. Boreham; *Some Reminiscences and Studies* by Robert Ferguson; *Calvary Clover* by E. H. Hobday; *None Other Name* by Ian Macpherson; *A Manual of Sermon Construction* by R. J. Wardell.

Faber and Faber for "The Universality of Jesus" by J. S. Stewart from *Modern Sermons,* edited by W. F. Stead.

Harper & Row for "In and Out" from *The Unemployed Carpenter* by Ralph W. Sockman.

Hodder and Stoughton for "What the Cross Nails Down" from *Call to Obey* by Murdo E. Macdonald; sermon outlines from *A Guide to Preachers* by A. E. Garvie; *If Any Man Minister* by E. D. Jarvis; *The Men Whom Jesus Made* by W. Mackintosh Mackay; *Sunrise* by G. H. Morrison; *The Spirit of Life* by

Tom Rees; *Life on the Uplands* by J. D. Freeman; *Sayings in Symbol* by David Burns; *The Three Crosses* by J. W. Falconer; *Forgiveness of Sins* by George Adam Smith; *The Four Men* by James Stalker; *A Man in Christ* by James S. Stewart.

David Hood for "The God of the Years."

Inter-Varsity Christian Fellowship for sermon outlines from *The Preacher's Workshop* by John Woods.

Light and Life Press for "The Duty of Forgiveness" and "The Danger of a Course of Sin" from *A Handbook of Homiletics and Pastoral Theology* by Wilson T. Hogue.

Mrs. James M. Macmillan for "The God of the Unexpected" and "Prayer and Efficiency" from *The God of the Unexpected* by Charles Frederick Wishart.

Marshall, Morgan & Scott for sermon outlines from *My Brother's Keeper* by Gerald B. Griffiths; *Walking on Two Feet* by A. Lindsay Glegg; *Life with a Capital "L"* by A. Lindsay Glegg; *The Life of a Christian* by John Macbeath; *Royal Sacrament* by Ronald A. Ward; *Heralds of the Gospel* by A. Skevington Wood; *God's Tomorrow* by J. Gregory Mantle.

The Monthly Record of the Free Church of Scotland for "The Victory of Faith" by G. N. M. Collins.

James Nisbet and Company for "Sin Finding Out" and "The Morning Star" from *The Work of the Ministry* by William Garden Blaikie.

Pickering & Inglis for "As a Tale That Is Told" and "The Supremacy of Character" from *Shoes for the Road* by Alexander Stewart; "Three Stages of Love" from *Outlined Bible* by Robert Lee; "The Fall of Belshazzer" and "Five Were Wise and Five Were Otherwise" from *Night Tragedies of Scripture* by R. J. Smithson; "Inseparable Things" by W. Graham Scroggie from *My Way of Preaching* edited by R. J. Smithson.

Fleming H. Revell for "Shifting Responsibility" and "Mistaken Estimate" from *The Bane and the Antidote* by W. L. Watkinson; "Successful Sin" from *The Supreme Conquest* by W. L. Watkinson.

Paul Sangster for "God's Greatest Gift" by W. E. Sangster from *Sermons I Should Like to Have Preached* edited by Ian Macpherson.

Charles Scribner's Sons for "What Can We Give God?" and "Giants and Grasshoppers" from *Sons of Anak* by David H. C. Read; "The Duty of Prayer" from *Theory of Preaching* by Austin Phelps.

Scripture Union for "Finding the Way" and "How People Hear the Word" from *Christian Living* by John Ellison; "Pauline Metaphors of the Christian Ministry" from *How to Illustrate Your Lessons* by J. Reginald Hill.

S.P.C.K. for "Every Barrier Down" from *The Creed and Its Credentials* by Lumsden Barkway.

James S. Stewart for "With God in the Dark" from *Sermons I Should Like to Have Preached* edited by Ian Macpherson.

Students' Christian Association of South Africa for "The Three-fold Ministry of Christ" from *The Holiest of All in Bible Sermon Outlines* by Andrew Murray.

Westminster Press and SCM Press for "Tetelestai" from *Teaching and Preaching the New Testament* by A. M. Hunter.

Zondervan Publishing House for "The Living Water" and "Spiritual Arithmetic" from *750 Sermon Outlines* by George W. Noble; "How the Thief Comes" from *The Second Coming of Jesus* by M. R. DeHann. Used by permission.

Index of Authors and Subjects

(References are to outline numbers)